How to Prune Almost Everything

How to Prune Almost Everything

by John Philip Baumgardt

drawings by Dorothy Chaisson

WILLIAM MORROW AND COMPANY, INC.
New York

Printed in the United States of America.

Library of Congress Catalog Card Number 68-11921

4 5 6 7 8 80 79 78 77 76

Contents

1. Why We Prune 7

maintenance pruning • pruning to recondition • hedge rejuvenation • shade and evergreen trees • fruits and vines • remedial and corrective pruning

2. How to Prune 17

what is your goal • how plants grow • some warnings • practice pinching • reworking a plant • removing a large limb • drop-pruning • special techniques • root-pruning • trench-pruning • tools and supplies

3. When and Where to Prune 41

winter and summer results • nature of buds and tissues • nature of roots • shade-tree schedule • fruit-tree schedule • evergreen timing • for perennials • continuous pruning

4. Special Techniques for Special Purposes 49

espalier-trained trees and cordons • topiaries • miniature trees and bonsai • for dramatic effect

A to Z of Pruning Plants 58

Abelia through Zizyphus: instructions for trees, shrubs, vines, tree and bush fruits, and perennials

Some Do's and Don'ts 186

Seasonal Guide 187

1 Why We Prune

The purposes of pruning are various: to keep plants healthy, to restrict or to promote growth, to encourage bloom, or to repair damage. Sometimes pruning is required to rejuvenate old, overgrown trees or shrubs; sometimes to encourage young plants to develop certain forms. Fruit growers prune to get bigger, better fruit and to prolong the life of their trees; rose growers prune for larger, finer blooms. Hedges are pruned to build up impenetrable growth. In every case, the purpose of pruning is to get more out of a plant.

Pruning is just one aspect of plant culture. Plants are cultivated, fertilized, watered, and they are also pruned. Too often pruning is looked upon as a mysterious technique to be undertaken by an expert. Nothing could be farther from the truth; pruning is just as much a part of everyday gardening as hoeing or mulching. Whenever you pinch back a petunia stem or cut a branch of forsythia for a vase, you are pruning. Pinching back the petunia stalk results in branching, and then more flowers. Cutting forsythia branches induces side shoots to break out below the cut and these will bloom next year. So it is that every gardener does some pruning even when he just removes spent blossoms, but the good gardener develops a conscientious pruning routine for the maintenance of his trees, shrubs, and woody perennials. Such pruning keeps them healthy, beautiful, and productive.

Maintenance pruning

Maintenance pruning varies from plant to plant but the goal is always the same: to enhance its ornamental value and to fulfill the purpose for which *you* selected it. Maintenance pruning involves removing flowers that are going to seed, nipping back vigorous new shoots so plants will branch low to keep their graceful shape, and periodically removing some basal shoots to encourage the development of an open, well-aerated, healthy crown.

Years ago, when the University of Missouri operated vast orchards through a division of its School of Agriculture, a student asked a professor, who was an active church worker, when was the best time to prune. "All but the fifty-two days of the year that fall on Sundays!" was his reply. And this is true. There is pruning to be done in every season. The beauty of Japanese gardens lies in their fine maintenance; in them, pruning is continuous, carried on with thumbnail and fingernail. Every new shoot is nipped at just the proper time to give plants the groomed look too seldom seen in our Western gardens. Perhaps the term "green thumb" came from the color of the pinching fingers of a good gardener. His thumb is indeed green, stained from plant juices as he frequently interrupts his other chores to nip back a shoot or pinch off a spent blossom.

Here are some examples of the need for maintenance pruning:

A young well-proportioned Pfitzer juniper planted near a sidewalk in a few years gets so big it must be removed or else be cut back so severely that its plumy grace is lost. A little yearly maintenance pruning could have kept it in hand and preserved its natural beauty.

A lilac bush from the nursery with three or four sturdy canes and a few smaller shoots apparently thrives untouched in the shrub border. Then in about five years it draws attention because it looks straggly, flowers are small, old trunks are insect riddled, and a host of weak, unbranched suckers crowd the crown keeping out sun and air. Regular pruning could have kept the trunk clean of suckers and the tops low enough to be seen.

The same with young privet plants set out for a hedge; not for two or three years are they sheared back. By that time they have developed a broad dense top supported by a few almost bare stalks. The effect is unsightly and the condition unhealthy. Yearly pruning would have produced thick growth, and, if the top had been kept narrower than the base, the low foliage would not have been deprived of light.

Fruit and rose growers are among the most faithful maintenance pruners. The fruit grower prunes to insure the fine quality yield on which his income depends; the rosarian prunes for flowers—a garden full of color or a mass of blooms to cut for the house. If you catch the

WELL-PRUNED ORNAMENTAL TREES. These white birches have been raised and thinned out by removing some of the lower branches. In the next few years the clump on the left will have a few inside branches higher in the tree pruned off to emphasize the beauty of the trunks. *Roche photo*

good rosarian in his garden without his clippers, it is only because his hands are full of spraying equipment!

There is not a plant that cannot benefit from regular pruning, maybe only removal of faded blooms, maybe thinning out. Maintenance pruning goes on throughout the growing season. And when you remove a twig or branch that droops—for a known or suspected reason—that's maintenance pruning, too!

Plants kept in prime condition seldom fall prey to pest and disease. For this reason alone maintenance pruning is important. Furthermore, plants that are kept shapely by fairly regular pruning seldom have to be severely overhauled and thus made unattractive for the year or so it takes them to recover their natural form.

Pruning to recondition

Sometimes the plants on your place appear to be doing so well, you fail to notice some great, overgrown, disease-ridden shrub that has gone its way, untended and unloved, for several years. Or you may have bought an old property where the neglected plantings have got entirely out of hand. Reconditioning presents formidable problems. The first one is, where to begin. Should you remove the great crop of spindly suckers crowding the crown or is it more urgent to get at those borer-infested, wrist-thick old trunks in the center? And how do you cope with the quantity of potentially floriferous but unbranched young wood that is entwined through the tangle of gnarled old trunks? This is the usual advice: First, remove all old and diseased wood; second, cut back promising healthy wood to encourage branching; and third, thin the sucker growth, retaining a few shoots to keep young wood coming on.

Don't work blindly. Get clearly in mind the purpose of steps one, two, and three. Then closely examine your problem shrub to determine how to proceed. You may not be able to take the steps in order; you may have to chop out some suckers (step 3) in order to get to the old trunks (step 1). These trunks will require a saw. To make room for the saw, you may have to sacrifice a few promising young shoots. My point is, get firmly in mind what you want the finished product, the pruned shrub, to look like, then begin to cut. But stop occasionally to walk around the plant; a shrub that has been pruned from one side only looks awful. Strive for balance and uniformity.

A reconditioned old shrub is apt to look sad indeed. Shorn of suckers, stripped of its crown of gnarled wood, with only thin unbranched young shoots remaining, it brings to mind the high school showerroom—just a crowd of naked, undeveloped striplings, exposed and unlovely. But the promise is there. Time favors the gardener, too, and his bush will also be handsome in the years to come.

PRUNING MAKES THE DIFFERENCE. Wrist-sized and larger branches, removed at Y-crotches, created this pattern of zig-zag limbs. Some branches, removed entirely, emphasize the character of the remaining ones, and these were cleaned of inner side branches. This is a masterful job of fitting a rigid, formal Austrian pine into an informal rock-garden setting. *Author photo*

Now some points on reconditioning; first as to the old wood. With deciduous shrubs, it is a poor idea to let any wood get so old it develops mature bark. But if you are faced with a shrub filled with gnarled, bark-covered trunks, reach for your pruning saw. Crawl among the trunks and work as close to the ground as you can. Cut off those old trunks right to the soil-line. Then paint the cuts with tree-wound dressing. It's no use cutting off old trunks at knee height or waist level. Take them out *to the ground* and do a clean job of it, sealing surfaces to ward off decay.

However, you may get into trouble if you wade in and heavily prune that fine old lilac your wife's grandfather planted. In just such an instance in one household, I observed a deep freeze set in and last for a week. If you are in such danger to peace of mind or bodily safety, drag out the job for two or three years; sneak out a main stalk to the ground now and again, and remove a few more suckers every time you feed the precious plant. It will be rejuvenated before anyone notices what is going on.

Handle with care the younger shoots, those with smooth, usually light bark. They will become the body of the plant for a few years while new wood is growing. Also cut down to the crown any shoots that are touching, any that are weak, diseased, insect-infested, or nicked by saw or loppers. Much depends on the species you are pruning, but it is good practice to space the shoots left to rebuild the shrub at least 2 inches apart, and farther if the crown is large.

Stop-back a few of these canes, making a clean angled cut just above a bud. Don't whack off all of them or the shrubs will take forever to assume a decent shape again. When you finish pruning, the remaining canes will look like sticks, but the light, let in by the spacing and removal of old wood, will soon cause buds to break up and down these stems, filling out the plant in a year or two. When a decision must be made whether or not to cut back the young shoots left on a rejuvenated plant, it is better to wait. Spacing is far more important than cutting back.

Finally, you have to cope with basal suckers left after the removal of old wood and the thinning out of new. Straight off, consider that any shoots coming from understock ought to be *dug out* and severed cleanly at their source. They are not often a problem, but occasionally "foreign shoots" appear from the understock of roses, flowering fruit trees, ornamental hazelnuts, and a few other groups of plants. Get rid of these as soon as they appear. On other root sprouts or suckers, use a sharp garden or tiling spade. Cut out all shoots that appear outside the desirable spread of the crown. Then thin the rest or, if buds are breaking from the crown itself, remove any shoots arising from below ground. Of course, a lot depends on the species and where it is growing. But a good rule is to leave a *minimum* of sucker growth.

Hedge rejuvenation

To bring back good looks to an old straggly privet hedge, just before leaves show in spring, cut it right to the ground or, at least, to very short stubs, say, to 8 inches. Accompany this treatment with fertilization, cultivation, watering—in fact, give your hedge the best of care—and a promising crop of new shoots will soon break from the old crowns. Shear these back through the summer and your hedge will rebuild itself in the course of two to three years. Old ericaceous plants—laurel, rhododendron, heathers—may be renewed in somewhat the same way. It is a poor practice to cut an old woody azalea or rhododendron to the ground, but you can safely remove as much as a third of the wood, leaving short stubs. New shoots will break from the old wood and, with feeding, mulching, and watering, the plant can be rejuvenated in about three years. Surprisingly enough, some species and cultivars of yew also respond well to such severe pruning.

Shade and evergreen trees

Specialists in tree care are frequently called upon to work over a valuable shade tree that has had no attention for years. First they

A WELL-TRAINED WISTERIA. Careful selection of stems that form the trunk, thinning out, and placement of lateral branches produce an ornamental vine heavy with bloom. As the clusters fade, it will be necessary to climb up and cut back all the new reaching tendrils, reducing each to one or two leaf buds, a job that will go on every two to three weeks through the summer. Here faithful pruning produces a handsome reward. *Roche photo*

FOR A SHADY LANE. Flowering dogwoods, planted close together, are trimmed high up for headroom. Since these trees resent stubbing back, all lower branches are regularly removed and high, natural crowns allowed to develop. (White birch and yellow-wood trees may be grown the same way.) For a more formal effect, the tops of the trees could be kept even and leafy by cutting back the upper branches every year or two. (For a *pleached walk* or allée, plant sycamore, poplar, apple, or some other species amenable to heavier pruning.) *Fred W. G. Peck, L.A.; Molly Adams photo*

remove all dead, weak, and interfering branches, cutting them back to a crotch or to a point where they break laterally from a main branch or trunk. Then the load of remaining branches is lightened by a technique called "drop-pruning"; this is described in Chapter 2.

Other techniques are often called for to insure the health of a tree. Limbs rising from weak crotches may have to be cabled together, cavities filled with mortar, patches of injured or dead bark "traced out," that is, removed back to healthy tissue. Then the resulting bare patch must be immediately sealed with tree-wound dressing. While you may be qualified to tackle some of this, where large tall trees are involved, professional equipment is required to reach the working areas and also to prune there *with safety*.

Little can be done to rejuvenate evergreen trees. They do not respond to branch or top work, and if lower limbs are gone, there is no way to replace them. The only way to assure the health and good looks of a fine blue spruce or specimen pine is to attend to maintenance pruning along with other good culture.

Multiple-trunked evergreens, particularly spreading junipers, arborvitaes, yews, and the like are something else again. Within reason, they can be reworked rather severely over a period of years. But never cut beyond *green* foliage. As long as there is a wisp of green, chances are it will grow to replace a branch that has been removed. But rejuvenating old spreading evergreens is a slow tedious process and scarcely worth while unless the specimens are valuable for reasons other than their obvious function in the planting.

Fruits and vines

Fruit-bearing plants need constant rejuvenation. A good pattern of maintenance pruning usually results in continuous replacement of old wood with younger, more productive branches. On cane fruits, most canes are removed as soon as they have borne fruit. With fruit trees, particularly apples, the present practice is to replant sections of an orchard from time to time rather than to depend on severe pruning.

Grape vines are cut back every year to just a few buds on year-old canes. This insures a good crop of fruit. With some ornamental climbers, it is desirable from time to time to renew them from the ground up. Trumpet-creeper, various ivies, honeysuckles, wisteria, and the more rampant species of clematis as they age can develop woody growth that endangers trellises, pergolas, roofs, even whole buildings. Very early in spring, rejuvenate such old woody vines by cutting them to the ground. With proper care they will renew themselves almost completely through the next growing season. Specific suggestions for pruning each of these are given in the A to Z section of this book.

Remedial and corrective pruning

Similar to pruning for rejuvenation is remedial pruning, which is concerned with repairing damage. A woody plant may be split by wind, by the weight of ice in a winter storm, or by a mechanical catastrophe, as being hit by a runaway car or a falling ladder (not to mention the painter who drops on the holly along with his ladder). Remedial pruning is a hurry-up technique aimed at saving a plant. Injured branches are cut back to a convenient crotch or trunk, and the cut is sealed with tree-wound dressing. Split trunks are pulled together, drilled, and bolted as quickly as possible to prevent entry of decay. Sprung limbs are somewhat lightened by removal of part of the terminal growth; then they are propped back into place until the injured wood regains strength.

Since remedial pruning is an emergency measure, you can't pay much attention to aesthetics. Better to save tree or shrub, battered and broken though it may be, than to lose it altogether. Just get to it as soon as possible after damage occurs. There is no set procedure. Clean up the mess and then, as growth is resumed, guide new shoots by judicious pinching and pruning so they will cover scars and stubs and eventually replace missing branches.

Corrective pruning is only slightly different. Perhaps a young shade tree persists in making its heaviest growth on the lee side, a common condition in windy areas. Branches on the "heavy" side of the tree must then be thinned and headed back to balance lesser growth on the windward side.

Some plants reach toward light, others reach toward a building. For example, in a mixed foundation planting, Japanese hollies soon lose form because they make most of the growth on the side away from the building. Meanwhile adjacent euonymous plants with a characteristic known as thigmotropism—that is, sensitivity to a solid body—grow toward the building and reaching shoots there become vinelike. In the case of the holly a little periodic thinning and heading back on the outside keeps the shrubs trim and balanced. With the euonymus, viny shoots growing toward the building are immediately removed, and the side of the euonymus toward the building is thinned out and cut back from time to time.

Sometimes the leader or main vertical shoot from an evergreen—a pine, spruce, or fir—is lost or damaged. To replace it, remove all vertical growth down to the highest whorl of branches. Then select the strongest lateral shoot and, by tying a stake to the trunk of the tree, pull the selected lateral into an upright position. In time, it will assume the form of the missing leader. To encourage dominance of this substitute leader, cut back the remaining side branches in the uppermost whorl, and continue to restrict their growth for two to three years.

WHEN NATURE PRUNES. The great American elm grows naturally to form this beautiful vase shape, which is unequalled by any other species. Crotches are nicely balanced; scaffold limbs evenly spaced, the crown delicately undulating. A garden specimen, crowded perhaps by other trees, the house, even by utility wires, may need help to achieve such symmetry. But cuts must be made with the greatest care and thought; one careless moment with a saw can destroy years of handsome growth. As always, the job of pruning is to work *with* nature. *Illinois Natural History Survey photo*

2 How to Prune

Pruning offers you a chance to practice second sight or, at least, foresight. Try to visualize the tree or shrub you intend to prune with the excess wood removed. Fix firmly in your mind's eye how the scaffold of your tree should look; then prune out the crowded internal wood, balance the crown, and raise the clearance. Get a good mental picture of your lilac bush with the mass of suckers and some of the oldest wood taken out, and then clean it.

My point is, have a clear goal when you begin to prune and work toward it. Work from all sides so the pruned plant will be symmetrical. Don't hurry! From time to time step back, refer to your mental image of the well-pruned plant, and compare it with the plant before you. As you become familiar with pruning techniques and patterns of plant growth, all this becomes automatic. But at first, take time to clarify your purpose before you make a single cut.

What is your goal?

When you shear a hedge, your goal is obvious—the maintenance of a dense, uniform barrier. The technique is to shape the hedge so light reaches the base on both sides. With this goal in mind, you will shear often enough to keep plants from looking ragged.

Flowering shrubs require two points of view: pruning for a fine crop of flowers and pruning for a plant that looks good in the garden even though it is out of bloom. You will remove tired old wood, weak wood, and most of the strength-sapping basal sprouts so that the young mature growth can have every advantage at flowering time. Such pruning does a lot for the looks of a shrub but you may also wish to lower the height a little by drop-pruning (as explained below) to keep a plant from outgrowing its place. If it is shaded on one side, a little corrective pruning may be necessary to bring the sunny side into balance. In any case, don't over-prune, or shear back tops alone for this will reduce your flowering shrubs to a cluster of sticks with broomy bunches of new shoots at the tips. It is true that from time to time the city gardener has to reduce his flowering shrubs rather drastically to keep them within bounds, but even so his annual pruning should be aimed at flower production and maintaining a shapely plant.

Fruit trees pose a problem. If you prune for fruit production alone, as the commercial orchardist does, you have to look at an unsightly tree for most of the year. On the other hand, if you do a minimum of pruning to make your apple, peach, or pear tree a nice garden ornament, you get smaller fruit. It's debatable but I favor the good-looking tree. After all, a small apple tastes as good as a big one if the tree is conscientiously sprayed to keep out worms. And you can avoid the problem entirely by planting dwarfed, espalier-trained, or cordon fruit trees. Then you add another element to your pruning goal, to keep plants from overgrowing. Here is where you "prune" with thumb and forefinger, pinching out new tips almost every time you pass your tree.

Prune your ornamental and shade trees in the way they want to grow. A weeping birch cannot be turned into the form of a Lombardy poplar no matter how much you cut back side branches. Your goal with trees is to strengthen them to resist wind and ice, to maintain ornamental form and good health. You might also prune for a lovely silhouette, for an open top to provide dappled shade below, or for some special effect. In the case of trees I would say that health and vigor come first.

With evergreens, prune to hold them to proper size and perhaps to thicken growth. Follow the natural form: Your Pfitzer juniper ought to be lacy and rather open, not sheared into a geometric form; your capitata yew ought to look loose and graceful, more like a hemlock than an oversized, green ice-cream cone. To keep your expensive evergreens looking like themselves you really have to use hand clippers and save the hedge shears for the privet. In a word, *naturalness* ought to be foremost in your mind when you pick up a pruning tool.

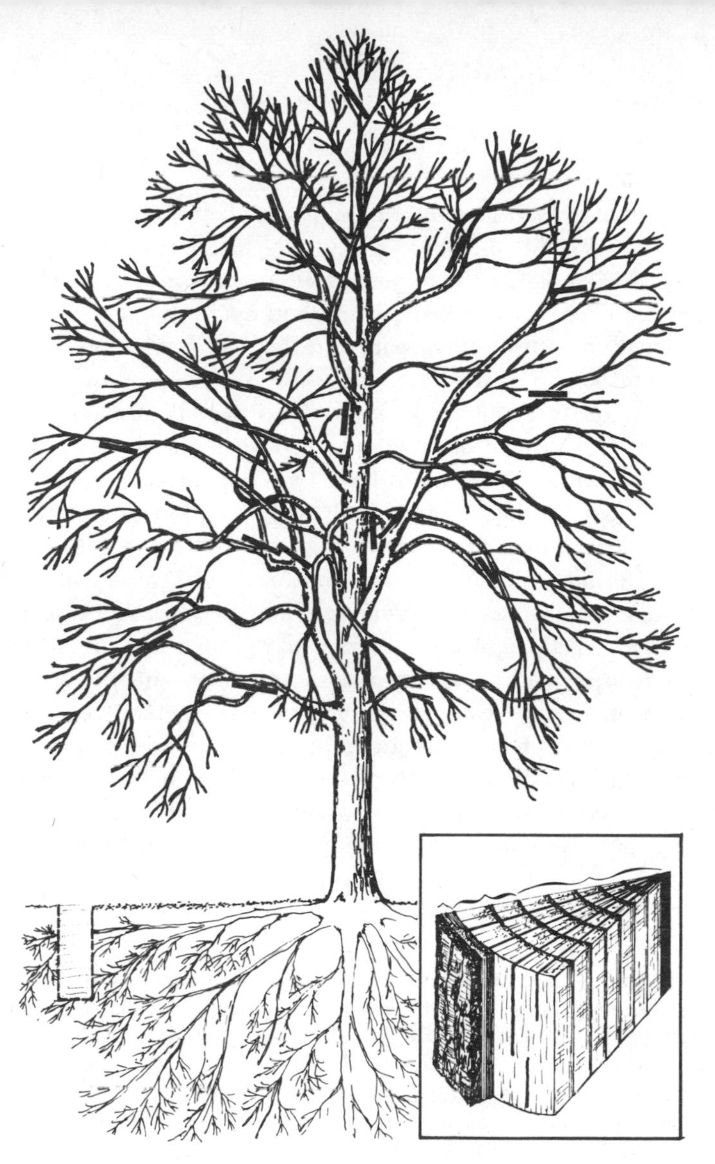

STRUCTURE GUIDES PRUNING. This typical tree is drop-pruned (Chapter 2), as shown, to control spread and to lighten the load at the ends of the branches. Crossing and weak branches are removed where they originate at the trunk. Root pruning is shown at lower left. A cut-away sketch of a tree trunk at lower right shows the layers of a trunk from the outside in: the hard protective bark, the soft bark that conducts sap and carbohydrates, the cambium where cellular increase occurs, the sapwood that conducts water and minerals mostly upward, and in the center the nonfunctioning heartwood.

How plants grow

As important as your goal in pruning is some knowledge of the growth habit of your plants. Look at an elm twig; notice that it is somewhat zigzag. That's because the terminal bud grows just a little to one side of the end of the twig; when the leaf bud opens, the new shoot is not quite lined up with the older part. But the bud of a horse-chestnut sits square on the end of the twig and so the shoots grow quite straight. Side buds on roses alternate with each other all around the stem; when you prune to an "outside bud," you force one shoot to grow just where you want it. Viburnums have two buds at each joint or node; when you cut just above them, both buds break to form new shoots.

Always try to prune to a bud because the part you cut off will be replaced by that bud, and no stub remains if you make a proper cut. Keep in mind that *all new growth comes from buds.* A plant gets taller from the tip upward, not from the ground-line or the middle. If you paint a mark 5 feet from the ground on an oak sapling and inspect it in twenty years when it has become a great tree, the mark will still be just 5 feet above ground.

Limbs and trunks get thicker as the layer of cells just under the bark, the cambium, makes new wood, also a little new bark each growing season. Important to the pruner is the cambium response when a branch is cut off. New tissues grow from all round the cut to eventually seal off the exposed wood. This is why it is essential to

HOW TO PRUNE A FORMAL HEDGE. At the left, proper pruning shapes plants, keeping them wide at the bottom, narrower at the top, thus admitting light clear to the base; if the lower part is shaded by bulging sides or a wide top, lower leaves and, eventually, lower branches are lost. The center diagram indicates a reasonable compromise, satisfactory for such vigorous growers as euonymus and boxwood. The diagram on the right shows bad pruning that will finally result in bare lower growth and a generally unsightly condition.

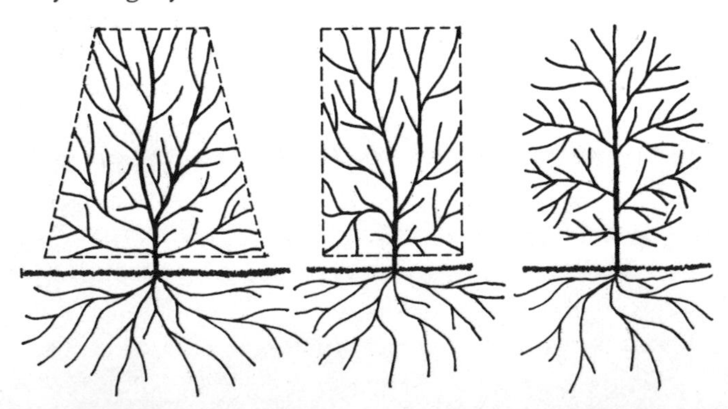

make a clean, smooth cut and why the cut must be sealed to keep out decay. Properly made and cared for, cuts heal over quickly and in a few years no trace remains.

Some plants, as forsythia and lilac, throw lots of new shoots from low in the shrub or from just under the ground. You can cut old wood back pretty freely on these shrubs and in a few years they will look the same as before. Other shrubs, as some viburnums and chokeberries, produce little basal growth so you must think twice before you cut a large cane clear to the ground. It's all a matter of knowing the growth habit of the shrub at hand.

Needle evergreens may be touchy about their uppermost shoot, called the "leader" or sometimes the "terminal shoot." If this shoot is lost, the tree may never regain its vertical tendency but growth will spread into an ungainly crown. You may safely *shorten* the leader of your pine, spruce, hemlock, and a few other sorts but never remove it entirely. At the same time, you ought to cut back a proportionate amount of the side shoots just below the shortened leader.

Keep in mind that plants grow from the tips of twigs upward, from the tips of roots downward, and that they increase in girth as tissue is added just under the bark. More on this later in Chapter 3.

Some warnings

If I hadn't scars to prove pruning mishaps, I shouldn't consider it necessary to warn you to keep your fingers out of clippers and away from saws. Good pruning tools are sharp and in many cases they have powerful leverage action. Don't get so interested in making a cut that you forget to keep *yourself* out of it! Let me give you some examples.

Clipping back bushy evergreens with hand-pruners offers a good opportunity to nip a finger. You work by grasping a bunch of tips with one hand, then reach in to cut away greenery beyond your hand. It's a good technique, the one the barber uses with your hair, and it does preserve the rippling surface of the evergreen. But if a finger in your "holding" hand sticks out rather than being clenched tightly around the evergreen, the clippers will catch it somewhere between the first joint and the end. Do wear heavy gloves when you are cutting rapidly and close to your hands, and keep your mind firmly on what you are doing.

Another danger involves hand-pruners with handles that curve in and meet at the back. When you are cutting a tough or oversized

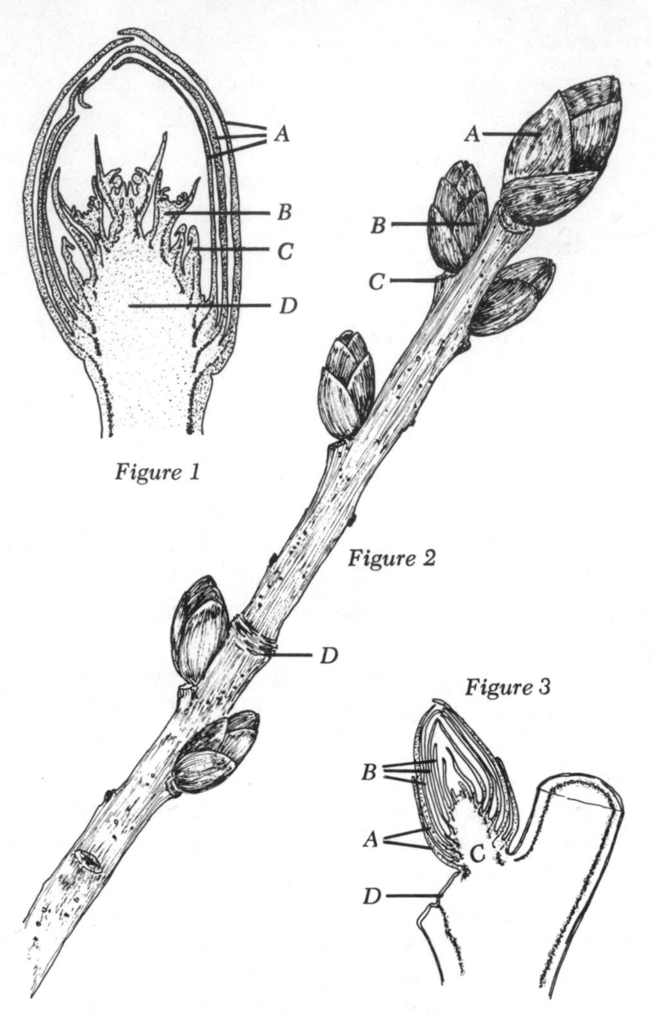

STRUCTURE OF BUDS AND TWIGS. Figure 1, a cut-away sketch of a dormant bud, shows A, bud scales; B, immature flowers; C, immature leaf; D, unelongated stem. Tissues in the stem D will stretch out lengthwise when sap flows in spring, and the bud will open, thrusting out the enclosed leaves and flowers. Figure 2, a sketch of a twig showing: A, the terminal bud; B, a side or lateral bud with C, a leaf scar just below it, where last year's leaf has dropped off (a bud is always just above, or in the axil of, a leaf). D, bud-scale scars, showing the location of last year's terminal bud (the section of the twig from this scarring on to the tip represents last year's growth). Figure 3 shows a lateral bud enclosing immature leaves but no flowers: A, bud scales; B, immature leaf; C, unelongated stem; D, a leaf scar just below.

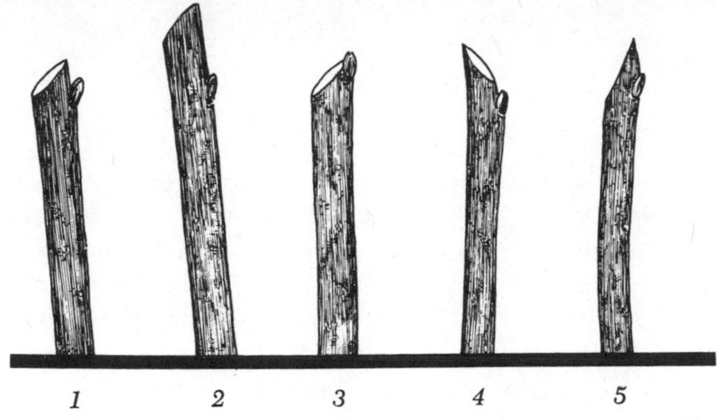

PRUNING CUTS CAN FAVOR A BUD. When a branch or twig is cut, there is good chance of decay. Make a clean, slanting cut just above a bud—regenerative tissues are active in this area and the cut will callus over quickly as a bud breaks to replace the shoot you have removed. Figure 1 shows the right place—a cut slanting away from the bud, and about a quarter-inch above it. In Figure 2 too long a stub is left. In Figure 3 too close a cut is made and the bud will probably be lost. In Figure 4 the cut is angled too sharply and slants *toward* the bud, leaving a blind tip. In Figure 5 the angle is too great and the cut is too far from the bud.

branch, it is a great temptation to get extra leverage by sliding your hand clear to the end of the handles. When the limb yields and the pruners snap shut, the fleshy portion of your hand is caught between the handle ends, and you get a huge blood blister to prove it. Try to avoid cutting branches too big for the tool.

Tree-pruning saws, so necessary in the garden, are just as wicked as they look. Good ones are curved to make the most of the to-and-fro action, and the great jagged teeth are designed not to be clogged by wet sawdust. Walk down the garden path swinging a pruning saw and you are bound to rip your pants leg if you don't gash your shin. Or use your free hand as a "guide" to align the saw when you start to cut and chances are you will snag the flesh in the crotch of your thumb if you haven't already caught a saw tooth in the quick of your first fingernail.

Almost every quality cutting tool comes with a sheath if you order it. For safety, keep your tools sheathed when not in use. Don't hang them bare on a nail or pegboard—they cut terribly when they fall—but lay them on a shelf. Don't test cut edges with your finger but on a leaf; only a sharp blade and properly adjusted cutting action can cut a leaf.

Keep your feet on the ground. Don't use wobbly stepladders, chairs, or other makeshifts to reach upper branches; it's dangerous; instead use long-handled pruners.

Practice pinching

You can avoid a lot of sawing, lopping, and hand-pruning if you practice pinching. A Japanese gardener, asked how he kept the garden so neat and trim, held up his stained and battered thumb and forefinger. When a bud breaks, it makes a stem with leaves along it. You can wait until it is tough and woody to cut it back and induce branching or, with less effort, you can pinch out the tip when the shoot has expanded to two or three leaves, and thus alter growth at that point.

When unwanted side shoots break from the cane you are training to a standard, you can wait until they are woody—but then they will leave scars where you cut them off—or you can rub off the buds as they appear. You can let your forsythia bush or any other woody plant overgrow or you can pinch back new growth early each year and almost avoid the use of cutting tools save for the regular removal of old or injured wood.

Pinching involves tender, rapidly growing tissues that can heal quickly with never a stub or scar. Nobody is going to pinch a barberry hedge rather than shear it but surely nobody should shear a rhododendron when growth is so easily controlled by pinching out terminal buds as shoots reach desired length. By all means become a pincher. Save your cutting tools for old wood and big jobs like hedges. As you walk around the garden, pinch out new growth here and there to control the development and shape of your plants. And this applies not only to "woodies" but to your perennials and annuals as well.

Reworking a plant

Once in a while a plant has to be reworked despite your best efforts at pinching and pruning. Too much old wood is present, perhaps too many wispy new canes shot up late last season, and the flowering wood is too long and unbranched. Or unnoticed a tree has grown too tall and broad and you realize that a big branch may swipe off your chimney in the first heavy wind. Or a beloved boxwood specimen has slowly enlarged until it almost covers the walk. When these things happen, we have to get out the tools and rework a plant.

Techniques are described in Chapter 1 under *Reconditioning,* and under *Remedial and Corrective Pruning.* Suffice it to say here that the quicker you get at the job the better. And when the plant is cut back, thinned, and a mere shadow of its former self, don't go off and forget it. New shoots will break soon, and you should be around to pinch

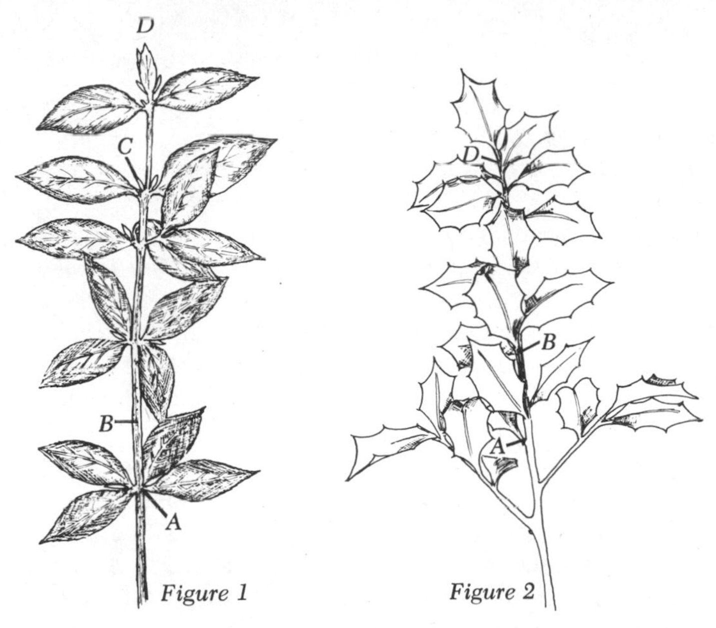

STRUCTURE OF LEAFY SHOOTS. Figure 1, forsythia, shows pairs of leaves at the nodes and clusters of leaves on stubby branchlets. Figure 2, American holly, has just one leaf at each node. In both: A, a node, the place where leaves and buds break from the stem. B, an internode, the area between two adjacent nodes. C, buds on the side of the twig in the leaf axil or angle called lateral or axillary buds. D, terminal bud, hidden in a cluster of rapidly expanding immature leaves. Holly also has latent buds, not visible to the naked eye, hidden under the bark of the internode. These dormant buds break out immediately behind a cut, so holly may be cut almost anywhere, not just at a node since a bud will break anywhere to replace the severed shoot.

them. If crowds of buds show up at the basal crown, use your gloved hand to rub off all but a few that are well spaced. And this also applies to new buds on the canes. As these open and new shoots break, pinch them at varying lengths so they branch and fill up the body of the plant. In other words, don't prune a plant heavily and then ignore it.

Removing a large limb

It's easy to get into trouble when you try to remove a large limb. If it is very large, say 4 or more inches in diameter, and also high up, it can be an awkward, even dangerous, job and you had better get a professional tree man to handle it. But most limbs under that size, you can cope with yourself. Nobody sits on the end of a limb anymore and cuts it off next to the trunk since comic strips have given that technique such play, but it is unbelievable how often people lean a ladder against the part to be removed and fall with the ladder when the limb goes.

Take down a large limb in sections to avoid tearing bark and cambium tissue. Such stripping is harmful to the tree and inevitably occurs when a partially cut limb falls of its own weight. If the sections are large, rope them first. Carry the rope through a crotch higher in the tree and tie it to a neighboring tree; then lower the pieces carefully. Any limb thicker than your wrist should be taken down in two steps.

First, undercut, that is cut up from the bottom, about a third of the way through the limb at a point 6 to 8 inches from the trunk. Next cut directly above, slightly beyond, or inside this first cut to drop the limb, leaving a stub on the tree. To remove this stub, undercut and then overcut it, working tight against the trunk. If the stub is more than 4 inches or so thick, you had better rope it to make cutting easier.

If you are very good with a saw and your two cuts were lined up well, the job is done. More likely you will need to use a draw knife to smooth the face of the cut and a heavy pruning or pocket-knife to whittle a smooth edge, beveling back the bark all round the wound. Finally seal the cut with tree-wound dressing. If the cut doesn't heal over in a year, reseal it each spring until it does.

Drop-pruning

This is a technique that calls for dropping or lowering your pruning cut to a crotch. Trees are drop-pruned when branches are too long or too heavy or when the crown is so dense that no light gets through to lawn or garden. Hard maples, lindens, and horse-chestnuts develop such dense tops that light is cut off and rain seldom penetrates the crown. Drop-pruning helps to reduce the hazard of breakage when limbs are overgrown and, on a smaller scale, the technique is used to lower branchy shrubs that have grown too tall. On trees not above 20 to 30 feet, say, you can probably do the job yourself. Before you get to work, examine the form of your tree or shrub.

Begin at the outer tip of a large limb and follow down toward the trunk; soon you come to a crotch; a little farther and there is another crotch and so on down to the main body of the limb. Sometimes the sides of a crotch are of almost equal size; sometimes one branch is much heavier than the other. Sometimes one side grows into the open

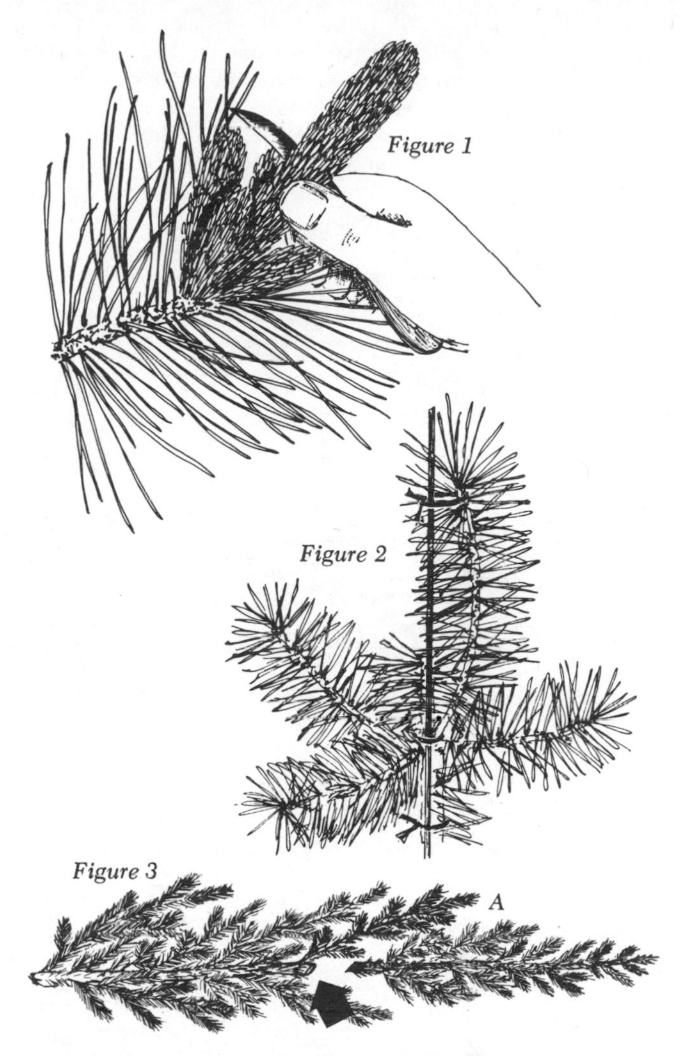

PRUNING AND TRAINING EVERGREENS. Reduce leggy growth and thicken up pines by removing new growth when it is about half grown as in Figure 1. Always keep the center "candle" a little longer than the ones clustered below it. If an evergreen tree loses its leader, or if the leader is injured, cut it out and, as in Figure 2, tie a bamboo stake into the tree with strips of soft cloth; then draw up one of the side branches and tie this in an upright position. In a year or two it will replace the missing leader. Figure 3 shows the right way to prune spreading junipers: Select a small shoot, A, lying on top of the branch and cut away the branch just beneath it, as indicated; the little shoot will replace the missing branch in a year or so. With this technique, you can control Pfitzer junipers without shearing them into unsightly green blobs.

PRUNING TOOLS. 1, Scissor-action clipper, or secateur, includes easily sharpened blades, a tension-adjusting nut at the base of the blades, and the accordian-type spring. 2, Smaller, needle-nosed secateur, useful for small twiggy plants, as miniature roses, perennial candytuft, small Japanese hollies, and the like. 3, American-designed clipper or secateur with a single blade working against an "anvil." 4, Hedge shears with serrated blades to grip twigs, a tension-adjusting nut, a shock-absorber device at the base of the handles, and rubber-cushioned grips. 5, Scissor-action lopper with strong, steel shanks and wooden grips. 6, Lightweight lopper with aluminum shafts and anvil action.

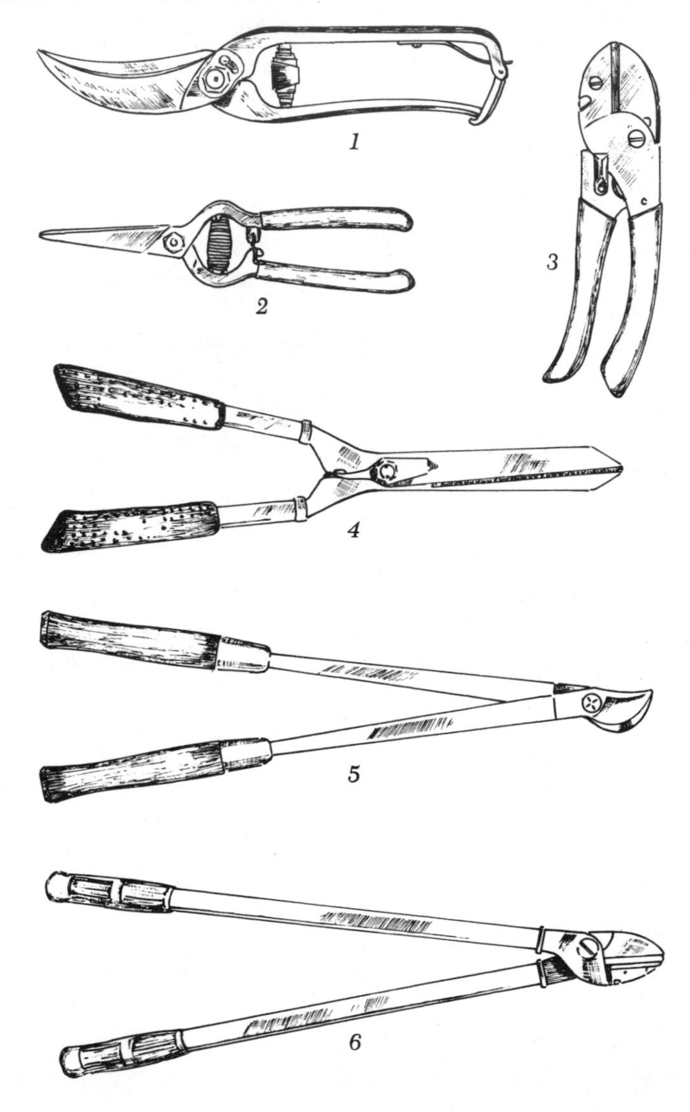

PRUNING SAWS AND SUPPLIES. 1, Folding saw, open and closed, for tight angles and small jobs. 2, Main pruning saw, well-designed with a fine steel blade, coarse teeth, and a slight curve to increase the cutting action for coarse shrub canes and tree limbs, will even cut down a sizable tree. 3, Pruning knife, open and closed, a useful but tricky tool for cutting back summer growth on trees, shrubs, and roses; if properly used, with a clean 45-degree cut just above a leaf, this does less damage than the best pruner, and the work goes faster. 4, Extension pole pruner, essential for tree work from the ground: a lever-action pruning hook removes branches up to an inch or so in diameter, and a detachable saw is useful for cutting larger branches. 5, Flexible leather or heavy canvas gauntlets to protect hands from bruises, scratches, and blade cuts. 6, Tree-wound dressing in an aerosol can for spraying any cut larger than a nickel. Before you store this, be sure to clear the nozzle by inverting the can with the spray on until no more liquid comes out.

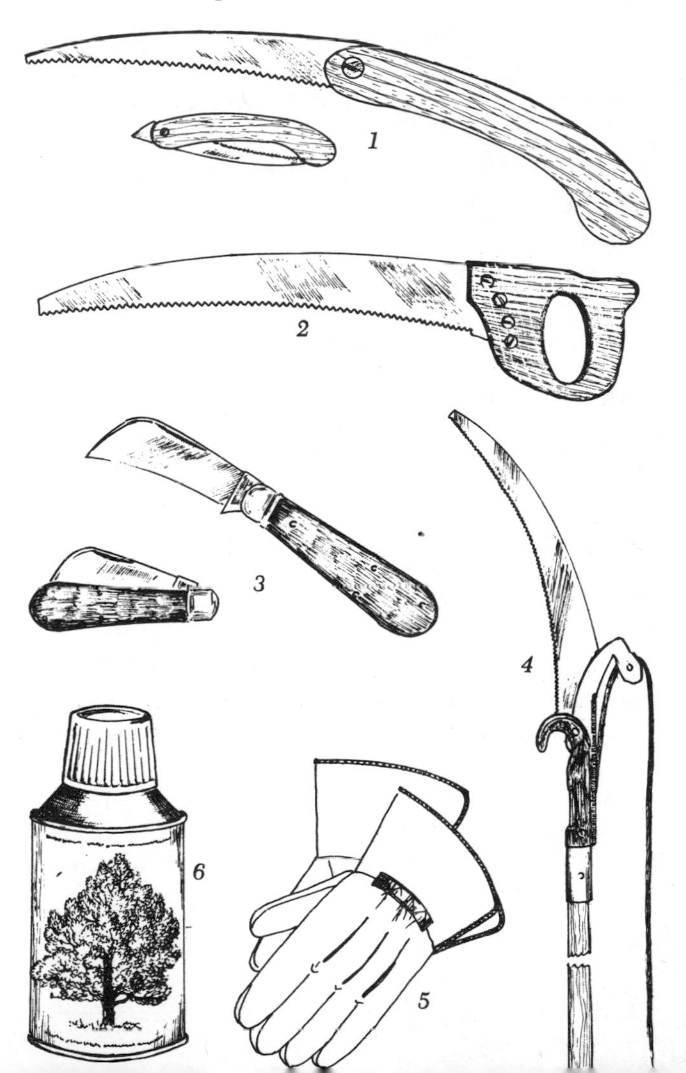

while the other crowds into a dense area in the crown of a tree.

You can cut off one of the two branches at the farthest part of a limb. In this way you can somewhat lighten the load of that limb and you may also relieve crowding. If you go deeper into the tree to make the cut at an inner crotch, you can take out a much bigger limb and make a larger opening in the crown. By drop-pruning, you can take out a few limbs high in the tree, a few more at crotches where limbs are 3 to 4 inches thick and, perhaps, even more branches down near the trunk where crotches are narrow and tight. A skilled arborist, pruning in this way, can remove as much as half the bulk of a large tree without altering its good appearance; the crown will simply look less dense.

Avoid leaving a stub when you drop-prune. Try to angle your cut on the limb you are removing so that it almost equals the angle of the limb you are saving. Again, if you are taking off large limbs and using a saw, work in two steps. Undercut first, then overcut, and finally smooth the surface of the cut, beveling the bark, and sealing with tree-wound dressing, as explained above in the directions for removing large limbs. Do call in a professional tree man for very large shade trees. These demand special climbing equipment, long-handled cutting equipment, and other paraphernalia, as well as more than average skill and judgment.

Special techniques

THINNING Evergreen *trees* are seldom thinned. Evergreen *shrubs,* such as spreading yews, Pfitzer junipers, and some upright growers have to be thinned from time to time if you are cutting them back each year to restrict their size. You recall that each time you cut off a limb, branches form below the cut; therefore, a shrub that is repeatedly cut back becomes so dense it may look artificial. Occasionally reach in below the crowd of branchy ends and take out a thumb-sized limb to break up the too even surface. Flowering shrubs, both deciduous and evergreen, have to be thinned from time to time, and this is a regular aspect of pruning. When you prune most shrubs, you remove old wood, reducing the crop of young shoots to just a few.

DEHORNING This inelegant term graphically describes a particular sort of tree butchery. Sometimes all the limbs of a large tree are sawed back—particularly at railroad stations—leaving great stubs sticking up. The trees are thus ruined since they will not regain a graceful branching system. We mention this technique only to remind you *never* to use it except as part of pollarding. Drop-prune instead.

POLLARDING Umbrella catalpas are a familiar example of this technique which results in a clean trunk with a cluster of year-old whips at the end of it. (A whip is a long, vigorous, unbranched shoot.) Pollarding varies from tree to tree and with your purpose. Pollarded sycamores may be allowed to develop naturally into sizable trees. Then the larger scaffold limbs are stripped of small side shoots and dehorned. Switches of new growth develop at the end of each stubbed limb and these are then cut back every winter. Regarded as desirable in Victorian times, this technique is still practiced in some European cities. If the pollarding is carried on close to the ground—that is with almost no trunk—the resulting bush is called a "coppice" and is recut almost to the original head every year or so.

PLEACHING Pleached trees formed bowers and arbors in castle gardens before Agincourt. Trees to be pleached are planted in close-set rows. Then limbs are pruned so they entwine to form a tight screen or wall; two adjacent rows may be trained over a system of arches to form a tunnel of greenery, or a ring of trees may be pleached to create a living summerhouse. A more ornamental way is to use two- or four-arm, espalier-trained trees set close so the branching system is more regular and attractive in winter.

LORETTE PRUNING This is a system used primarily for high production of table pears but it is applicable to other fruits. It is a refined method requiring knowledge of the development of fruit-bearing structures on the limbs and confined to summer manipulation. The object of the system is to force the development of so-called "stipular eyes"—those tiny dormant buds near the base of new shoots—*by removing the shoot just above these eyes* as soon as it is pencil-thick and becoming woody. This is an over-simplification but it gives you an idea of the procedure.

In April, shoots that extend the branches are shortened to about two-thirds or even half, depending on their vigor; this forces buds below on older wood to break and make lateral shoots. In mid- to late June, these lateral shoots are cut back. The timing depends on their having reached the necessary pencil thickness and having developed a woody core. They are cut to within half an inch or less of their base. Usually a leaf or two is left, sometimes not, depending on the type of woody structure below the shoot being reduced. In July, shoots that were not sufficiently developed at the June pruning are cut back. Again in September late maturing shoots are reduced to stubs; at the

A GOOD GRIP, A GOOD TOOL, AND A GOOD CUT. The hand-pruner removes a twiggy stick thus forcing succulent shoots below to develop more quickly. Pinching out the tip of the shoot just below the blade will encourage tight branching. *Philpott photo*

same time secondary shoots, resulting from the severe early pruning, are cut to one fruit bud.

As a result of this drastic summer pruning the stipular eyes, which may have remained dormant for years, develop into "dards" with fruit buds during their first season. An unbelievable number of flowers are thus produced all along the branches. Ultimately these flower-bearing dards develop into fruit spurs with a long productive life.

Lorette pruning is most effective on espalier-trained and cordon trees. The fruit on well-grown Lorette-pruned trees is of exceptional quality and is borne in quantity. If you are growing dwarf trees or trained trees, by all means visit the library and read *The Lorette System of Pruning* by Louis Lorette, published by John Lane, The Bodley Head Ltd, London. You could become the pear magnate of your town!

Root-pruning

Everyone talks of pruning the tops of trees and shrubs but almost no one mentions whacking back a few roots. Yet how logical root-pruning becomes when we think of it in terms of growth control. Top pruning removes excessive growth, but why not prevent the development of such growth by removing enough roots to inhibit top development? In this view, root-pruning becomes a worthwhile technique.

But it is not an easy technique. You cannot see the pattern of the root structure. It is difficult to tell just where the roots are down in the soil and how many you can cut away without doing a plant in completely. Root-pruning requires care and some experience.

In general, root-pruning has two functions: to shorten, for a season or two before transplanting, the long roots and encourage the production of a thicker system on such sparsely rooted plants as dogwood, sour gum, older redbuds, many evergreens, and some fruit trees, as apple, plum, and pear, to control excessive top growth on espalier-trained and cordon trees. The recent introduction of understocks that are less apt to produce excessive leafage has limited the need for much root-pruning on fruit trees. But root-pruning is a useful technique when you are faced with a flowering crabapple that seems determined to take over your whole garden or an espalier-trained fruit tree that produces new growth in feet rather than inches.

To root-prune a young tree, dig it up in late fall just before leaf drop. Cut back to varying lengths the oldest, heaviest roots, making clean, slightly diagonal cuts. Almost entirely remove any roots growing straight down. Shorten spreading roots by as much as a half. Leave intact well-branched roots and small roots. Then quickly replant the tree before the exposed roots have a chance to dry out. Add moist organic material—leafmold or crumbled peatmoss—to the soil and ram this mixture firmly round the roots with a post or tamper. To prevent its being worked loose by the wind, stake the tree immediately.

Trench-pruning

Older trees can be pruned in place by trenching. With a fork dig about a 15-inch-deep trench halfway round a tree at some distance from the trunk, usually about two-thirds of the way out toward the ends of the branches. Carefully push aside the small, fibrous roots that are to be saved, cleanly sever the old, woody, unbranched roots, and pull out the cut ends. These should not be left to decay in the soil. As in simple root-pruning, work humus into the soil, filling the trench a little at a time and ramming the soil mixture down tight.

Guy the tree, that is, wire it in place to prevent rocking in the wind.

REWORKING AN OLD FRUIT TREE. Here is the final step in removing a large limb growing crosswise into the center of a tree. The cut is made with a bow-saw, a handy tool for orchard work and general tree pruning. The saw blade has coarse teeth that are not choked by wet sawdust. Note that here the second cut is made nearer the trunk than the first cut, not beyond as in the later photograph, "Removing a Limb." Either placement of the second cut prevents stripping of bark. The orchardist, as in this picture, seems to favor making the second cut *behind* the first, while the forestry man and commercial arborists make it *ahead. Flower & Garden photo*

The other side can be root-pruned the next year. The second pruning may be unnecessary but in some cases it is required. If you have to make a second trench, burrow in under the tree and cut the heavy roots that grow straight down just below the crown. Gardeners in mild, misty climates where soil is deep and rich appreciate this necessity.

When preparing a sparsely rooted tree or shrub for moving, trench halfway around the tree as if a ball were being cut for transplanting. A good rule of thumb is to allow a 3- to 6-inch radius of undisturbed root for each inch of trunk diameter. Cut all roots halfway round and cut in under the tree at the same time. Refill the trench with a half-and-half mixture of soil and damp organic material, as leafmold or brown, not black, peatmoss. Add a small amount of bonemeal or superphosphate to stimulate production of fibrous roots. The next year perform the same operation on the other side of the tree. Then lift the tree and move it the following spring, digging just outside the circular line of the original trench. (For a tree with a 4-inch diameter trunk, the circle cut around the root area would measure 12 to 24 inches across.)

Sometimes young espalier-trained apples, tending to overgrow, can be brought under control with somewhat less commotion. I have sometimes used a razor-sharp tiling spade to make almost vertical cuts, more or less hit or miss, in a semicircle around the trunk of a tree. When I strike a root I pry it up and pull out the severed end. Twenty minutes effort usually result in moderate growth the next season. When pruning roots, you need not apply wound dressing to cut ends so long as cuts are clean and the plant is in good health. Severed roots callus over almost immediately and heal quickly. It has been claimed that the presence of wound-dressing chemicals in the restricted atmosphere of the soil inhibits the production of fibrous roots; however, considerable research would be required to substantiate this.

REPAIRING TREE-TRUNK INJURY. If your tree develops dead patches of bark due to disease or insect infestation, or if the bark is torn and bruised by mechanical injury, use a sharp knife to "trace back" to tight, healthy bark. Avoid scalloped edges. Scrape the exposed wood until it is smooth or, if it is decayed, cut to clean, healthy wood with a chisel. Seal exposed wood and bark edges with tree-wound dressing. Redress each year until the wound heals over. *Illinois Natural History Survey photo*

REMOVING A LIMB. Make the three cuts shown to avoid ripping bark. Number 1 is an undercut some 12 inches from the trunk. Number 2 is a downward cut made above and just a little beyond the first cut, as here, or a little inside it, as in "Reworking an Old Fruit Tree." In any case, the first two cuts remove most of the limb and take a lot of weight from the stub. Number 3 severs the stub with a clean cut. *Illinois Natural History Survey photo*

Tools and supplies

To do your own pruning, you need a few special tools.

A CURVED PRUNING SAW with a 9- to 15-inch blade and medium coarse teeth is essential for limbs and canes of more than 1½-inch thickness. Don't buy the larger saw meant for removing large limbs because it won't fit into a crowded clump of shrub canes, and don't buy the special double-sided model until you have had quite a lot of experience. With it you might find yourself cutting out three or four desirable canes along with the one or two you wished to remove.

A LOPPER is necessary for cutting woody stems of ½ to 1½ inches in diameter. Buy a lopper with long steel shanks; all-metal handles are even better. A shock absorber is not essential but it helps to protect wrists and hands if you have a lot of lopping to do. The best lopper you can afford is a bargain in the long run; low-cost models spring after a few heavy cuts and the blades crush and mangle rather

POLE PRUNER AND EXTENSION SAW. With this double-use tool, you can stand on the ground and drop-prune young shade and fruit trees or saw off smaller branches. If you are using the hook pruner, above, take off the removable saw blade to keep from skinning nearby twigs—it was left on here to show the whole tool. The small sharp saw on the extension rod makes high-up work possible without the use of a wobbly ladder. *Seymour Smith & Son, Inc. In Use photo*

than cut. Or the handles buckle on a heavy cut and your knuckles are smashed in the process. There is no such thing as a good lightweight lopper; the heavier they are, the better. A pair of aluminum handled loppers is now in my trash can. They are beautiful—red plastic grips, aluminum shafts, and light "steel" blades with a shock absorber. They lasted through the hollow stems of one large forsythia bush and bit the dust on the third small trunk in the plum thicket.

You need at least ONE HAND-PRUNER OR CLIPPER, a "secateur," for small pruning. Choose one that suits your hand and be assured a cheap clipper is also no bargain for the blades soon spring, and instead of making a clean cut, they mash stems. Test the latch and the grip before you buy. You are sure to find a favorite; then keep it in a safe place away from casual borrowers. I value my German Henkle secateur with scissor action. It is of simple construction, rugged—in constant use for nine years—and can be serviced, if necessary, by any good cutlery shop. If you buy a clipper with *blade-and-anvil action,* get the best and plan to return it to the manufacturer from time to time for adjustment. You could also use a second pruner with good *scissor-action* on the tender stems of roses, clematis, and the like that may be crushed by the anvil-type pruner.

A PRUNING KNIFE is handy once you get the hang of using it for nipping back soft shoots, vine tendrils, and other succulent growth. Get a folding model like a pocket knife. I favor one with a heavy blade that is slightly hooked like a linoleum knife. This is also a useful tool for cutting back raspberry canes, rose canes, summer shoots on fruit trees, new growth on clematis, and other soft tissue. Keep it sharp and clean.

A HEDGE SHEARS is necessary if you have a hedge and, possibly, a POLE PRUNER if you grow fruit trees. Later, you may want a POLE SAW, a HEAVY-DUTY SAW, a POWER SHEARS, even a CHAIN SAW, but these are not essentials for the average garden. Better concentrate first on buying a few first-rate hand tools.

In addition to cutting implements, you need a SPRAY CAN OF TREE-WOUND DRESSING and also some PASTE DRESSING for use on windy days.

Do make a habit of cleaning your tools when you bring them in. Wash your saw blade after use with kerosene. If necessary, remove any gummy deposit with steel wool, and rub blades with light machine oil before storing. Rub off sap and gum from all your tools and wipe them with an oily rag before slipping them into their sheaths or laying

A CURVED PRUNING SAW with a 9- to 15-inch blade and medium coarse teeth is essential for limbs and canes of more than 1½ inch thickness. The larger sized saw is meant for removing large limbs and won't fit into a crowded clump of shrub canes; the special double-sided model is not for you until you have had quite a lot of experience. With it you might find yourself cutting out three or four desirable canes along with the one or two you wish to remove. This smaller, curved pruning saw has many uses in the home garden.

HEAVY-DUTY SAW. For this small maple limb a single, direct cut will do. Let your free hand steady the branch so the final strokes of the saw are smooth and the limb does not fall away, pulling a strip of bark with it. The serious gardener with many trees needs at least two pruning saws, a straight-bladed one like this and a smaller one with a curved blade (rigid or folding into the handle) like the one above for general use. *Seymour Smith & Son, Inc. In Use photo*

FIT THE TOOL TO THE JOB. Use this lopper to cut the smaller viburı cane, but a larger, heavy-duty pruner or a pruning saw for the thi wood. The cut is made as close to the ground as possible and slaı slightly for drainage. *Seymour Smith & Son, Inc. In Use* photo

them on that special, uncrowded shelf. If blades get dull, better them sharpened by an expert at a cutlery shop. Or send back y best tools to the manufacturer for servicing; the charge is nominal.

3 When and Where to Prune

To do a good job of pruning you need to know a little about plant physiology and why pruning sometimes stimulates growth, sometimes retards it, or, at least, does not cause the production of new shoots.

Winter and summer results

Winter pruning results in a burst of strong spring growth: when the proportion of top to root is decreased, the flow of sap feeds the remaining top to capacity, and buds burst forth. Summer pruning inhibits growth. Since leaves make food for the entire plant, the removal of leafy branches reduces the amount of food produced, and replacement growth is consequently much less vigorous. For example, if in winter, you remove considerable wood from the top of trees, in the spring, long, succulent shoots or water sprouts will be produced along the main limbs and perhaps also from the trunk. But if you prune your tree the same way in summer, fewer sprouts will be produced and, if you remove these immediately, they are unlikely to be replaced.

This is the way it works. New shoots come from buds. If you peel open a bud under a microscope, you will see that it contains tightly folded leaves and perhaps flowers. When a bud opens, it is rather like the pulling out of a telescope: spaces between leaves (internodes) elongate, leaves expand, and a new shoot—with or without flowers—is ready to grow and eventually harden into a woody branch.

If you cut back a branch, buds just below the cut are stimulated and one or more shoots soon start to grow. Here we see one good reason for drop-pruning, the technique of removing limbs *at their source.* If you try to open up and lighten the top growth of a tree by stubbing back branches, more wood will grow back than you removed. But if you drop-prune, thus removing some branches entirely and leaving others to absorb the sap flow from the roots, few if any buds will break, although the tip growth on the remaining branches may be somewhat enhanced. To force trees and shrubs to branch, we take advantage of this phenomenon of buds breaking *below* a cut. So it is that we induce branching when we cut back a stem, when we shear a hedge, even when we pinch out the tip of a shoot.

Nature of buds and tissues

Buds are classified by content and location. Some buds are flower buds; some buds contain both a shoot and the start of a flower; others are strictly vegetative, containing only a shoot. Flower buds are usually round and plump, larger than vegetative buds, which tend to be pointed and less "stuffed" looking. When you prune grapes, bush fruits, and fruit trees, you need to recognize the difference between flower and fruit buds. Then you can control the set or amount of fruit through the number of buds you save.

Buds at the tip of a stem are called "terminal" buds; when they open, they extend a branch. Buds along the sides of a branch are called "lateral" or "axillary" buds, axillary because they lie in the axil of the leaf, the angle where leaf joins stem. When axillary buds break, they form side or lateral branches. We can force axillary buds to make a shoot by cutting off the stem just above them. Since the bud will make a branch in the direction it faces, we can pretty well control the shape of a plant by pruning at selected buds.

Sometimes buds are latent or hidden in bark or folds of tissue. We can't see them but they are there, ready to grow if the shoot beyond them is lost or removed. Latent buds break easily in some species. For example, you can cut a holly, azalea, or yew branch almost anywhere and small bumps along the remaining branch will soon indicate the activity of latent buds. From them, new shoots will be produced below the cut in a few weeks.

Roots have no buds. If a root is severed, new growth starts from deep within the core. Branch roots are produced from inside the body of the root, rather than from the surface, as in the case of buds on stems and branches.

MAGNOLIAS PRUNED FLAT. This pair of evergreen shrubs, through pruning, is used to accent an entrance. The masses of glossy green foliage, well-controlled, formal, yet not *too* formal, look just right on the high brick wall. Tips of out-growing branches are pinched back several times through spring and summer, and a branch removed here and there to let the brick show through. Grown this way, trees require little fertilizer; if new growth gets leggy with long spaces between leaves, root-prune a little. This *Magnolia grandiflora* is hardy to St. Louis, has even been successful as a wall plant at Niagara Falls. *Molly Adams photo*

Bud dominance

Certain buds influence the growth of the buds *below* them by producing growth-inhibiting substances that move down the stem and prevent nearby buds from breaking. We call this "bud dominance." In most shade trees, there is little bud dominance. While three or four buds below the terminal bud may remain dormant, others farther down eventually grow.

In pines, spruces, firs, and some other evergreens, "apical" or tip-bud dominance is more pronounced. Few buds break near the top and growth there is limited; farther down the trunk, growth is more vigorous. The result is a typical cone-shaped plant. But palm trees have complete apical-bud dominance. They never branch. Lateral buds are so inhibited that even when the terminal bud is removed, side buds fail to break and the tree dies.

There are practical uses for this information. Keep in mind that when you remove a terminal bud from a plant with tip-bud dominance it may die, since new shoots will not start below due to the inhibiting influence. Only a few entirely unbranched tropical species behave this way. In most trees, there is little such dominance, and the removal of a terminal bud results in active growth and the making of many new shoots below, often detracting from the appearance of a tree. Thus drop-pruning is often the best procedure for shade trees.

When a bud opens and expands, it leaves a stem behind it. While this is soft and green, it contains only the tissues that were formed by a small cluster of embryonic cells buried at its very tip. Later secondary tissues are produced by a cylindrical layer of cells separating wood and bark. This is called the "cambium." Every spring the cambium produces a fresh batch of wood cells; as summer wears on, these become smaller and fewer for dry soil and heat slow down vital processes. By fall, all growth ceases.

If you cut across a branch, you can see these rings of cells. They are the ones that in maturity make the pretty patterns in wood used to make furniture. Newly produced wood cells conduct water and minerals from the soil to the upper parts of a tree. Other cells are produced by the cambium to make bark. Outer bark is hard and dry, the cells are dead. Inside, adjacent to the cambium, the bark is soft and active, carrying sap enriched by carbohydrates down from the leaves to feed trunk and roots.

In roots the situation is different. Conducting tissues start out deep inside the root. As the root ages, it develops a cambium that produces secondary tissues like those of the trunk. When you prune trees and shrubs, you disrupt normal channels of sap flow and expose vital tissues to infection by bacteria and fungi. That is why you use tree-wound dressing to seal off fresh cuts as you make them.

As for how plants "breathe," actually, they don't, but oxygen, carbon-dioxide, and other gases diffuse in and out of leaves and young shoots through special openings. Pruning does not seem to upset the functions of normal gaseous exchange in plants.

Shade-tree schedule

Large shade trees and most ornamentals, such as crabapple, Japanese

PRUNING IVY ON THE HOUSE. In this formal treatment, the vine is clipped over with a hand-pruner once a month through the growing season to maintain the rigid pattern. The bony look of exposed stems can be avoided by letting a few tendrils grow to cover them. For a less formal effect, simply head-back new shoots that adhere to the brickwork; cut back any dangling tags at the same time, and keep the ivy away from window frames and other woodwork. *Roche photo*

pagoda-tree, and weeping mulberry, may be pruned at almost any time. Only a few, such as birch, maple, and walnut bleed if pruned late in winter or early spring, and specific warnings for these are given in the A to Z section. General shaping and storm repair can be done in winter. Then you can remove branches that are too low —we say that the crown is raised—and also take out crowded and interfering limbs. Wait until leaves open to lower a crown for protection from wind; with branches clad, it is easier to see what you are doing when you attempt to balance out the top of the tree. At the same time, remove dead and weak wood for it is easily identified when trees are in leaf. Let the elm retain its natural crotches.

Fall is the best time for root work. Watch for girdling roots, those that curl around the base of a trunk. As they increase in size and the trunk also grows larger, they restrict the flow of sap up the trunk just as a tourniquet restricts the flow of blood through your arm. Cut off girdling roots where they originate; also remove excessive surface roots, and roots that pry up sidewalk or driveway. To lure roots down into the ground, deep-feed trees that keep making surface roots.

Fruit-tree schedule

For the fine points of pruning for fruit production in your area, apply to your County Agricultural Extension Agent (also called Farm Adviser or County Agent) at the county seat. He can supply both pamphlets and special advice. You may wish to use the Lorette system for your pear and apple trees or the more usual techniques. These are explained for each kind of fruit tree and bush fruit in the A to Z section. Just look up your fruit there for specific information.

Evergreen timing

Prune most of the cone-bearers and related sorts, such as yews, when new growth is fully expanded but before it has hardened. New shoots on pines are called "candles." Use a sharp knife to cut these off halfway or less, but always leave the center candles at the top of the tree and at the end of each branch a shade longer than the ones that surround them. Never remove old limbs from tree evergreens for they will not be replaced. If you cut back *below* green needles, chances are no buds will break, and the gap where you took out a branch will remain forever. Throughout the growing season, you can freely whack at bushy evergreens, such as spreading or creeping junipers, most yews, and most arborvitaes.

FOR MODERN ARCHITECTURE. *Now* the rhododendrons and azaleas are low, perfectly suited for their setting below a picture window; left untended for ten years they will reach the eaves. *Now* the young dogwood is thin and lacy; unpruned for a few years, it will develop a dense, formless crown. Each new shoot on the shrubs should be pinched back to two leaves and, occasionally, a branch cut out here and there to avoid a too-even look. To preserve the delicate, open look of the dogwood, some thinning out is required every year. *Molly Adams photo*

Folks seem to overdo or underdo the pruning of foundation evergreens; either they shear bushes into unnatural, geometric shapes or let them grow to engulf both house and sidewalk. Plant young evergreens far enough apart to allow for growth; then begin pruning right away. As they fill allotted spaces, prune harder. Early in summer, use the loppers to reach in and take out one or two sizable limbs and cut new growth back hard. Do this throughout the growing season, finishing up perhaps with a pre-Christmas trimming to have evergreens for the house. Avoid pruning woody plants late in winter or early in spring. At the end of this book, you will find a brief Seasonal Guide for quick reference.

For perennials

Pinching and pruning are aspects of perennial culture, often prolonging bloom and, with the tall, late growers, avoiding staking. Early perennials such as delphinium, columbine, hollyhock, and lythrum are not pinched but let bloom. Then the spent stalks are pruned off to the basal rosettes of leaves or to a low point on the stem where branching is apparent. In this way, a second crop of flowers may be brought on.

Pinch tall-growing, later-flowering perennials, as chrysanthemums, hardy asters, summer phlox, heleniums, Michaelmas daisies, and golden-glow when they have made five to six leaves; pinch again when the resulting branches have made about the same number. Do this before stems are hard or spindly. This technique produces lower, bushier plants that will usually stand alone. However, keep in mind that the more branches you force, the more bloom you will have, but the bushier the plants the smaller the flowers. With phlox, I like a clump pruned to four main stems. I let one go unpinched, pinch back one stalk about May first, another about mid-May, and the last on June first. This gives large heads and extends blooming time.

Of course, with chrysanthemums particularly, it does no good to pinch if clumps are not divided in spring, but even good divisions come to nothing if they are not pinched out to form a well-branched plant. Tweak off the soft vegetative tips when growth is 4 to 6 inches high, and then when it has increased that much again. For early bloomers, stop pinching by mid-July, and late ones by August first.

Remove spent flower-heads from all perennials before seed is formed. This prevents weakening the parent plant. It also avoids having seedlings clutter up the beds, usually with undesirable progeny.

Continuous pruning

In warm climates, as southern California, tropical Florida, and along the Gulf Coast, the answer to "When to prune?" is "Always!" Where growth goes on all the time and there is almost no period of dormancy, great effort is necessary to keep plants in bounds, to maintain open ornamental forms, to have shadows on the lawn instead of deep shade. Unlike plants in temperate climates with cold winters, most of those in warm regions need "continuous" pruning.

Of course, not all tropical plants develop the same way. For example, while Japanese euonymus and myrtle grow more or less steadily, other true tropicals, as citrus trees and most flowering species from tropical Australia, show definite seasonal behavior. When necessary, seasonal ones are heavily pruned at the ebb of active growth, but light pinching and flower cutting go on through the growing period.

4 Special Techniques for Special Purposes

In Europe and Asia, less often in this country, one purpose of pruning is to create such artificial forms as fans, cordons, and espalier-trained trees, particularly for fruits. Topiary pruning of certain shrubs produces fanciful figures of birds, animals, or geometric figures. Then there is the Oriental technique of pruning trees to restrict growth and create the look of gnarled and aged specimens, as in bonsai. In a garden, imaginative pruning of a well-placed tree can produce a dramatic specimen as a feature or accent.

Espalier-trained trees and cordons

An espalier is a trellis fixed to a wall for the support of a plant, which is pruned flat to the trellis. As a rule, lateral branches are trained to a symmetrical pattern. In northern Europe, fruit trees are grown on espaliers to insure a crop of peaches or of the soft, aromatic, dessert pears. Modern gardeners appreciate the space-conserving and ornamental values of espalier training and apply the technique to various plants, such as dwarf fruit trees, French hybrid cultivars of *Ceanothus,* of flowering quince—particularly the Chinese strains —cotoneasters, forsythias, pyracantha, yews, and some of the semi-deciduous, fragrant-flowered viburnums. The plain, often stark, walls of modern architecture offer good surfaces for espalier-trained plants.

You get the most satisfactory results if your fruit trees are on *very* dwarf rootstock and other plants are of dwarf strains or naturally slow growing. Avoid trying to develop espalier-trained specimens from such vigorous or uncooperative plants as standard fruit trees,

ESPALIER-TRAINED PEAR TREE. This well-shaped tree is now in need of a little corrective pruning. The out-of-place, upright trunk springing from the lower lefthand scaffold limb should be cut out; lateral branches throughout the tree should be cut back to two or three leaves, and the broomy clusters of twigs at the top reduced to one or two short branchlets on each upright limb. It takes time and continuous, careful pruning to maintain an espalier-trained tree. *Molly Adams photo*

honeysuckle bushes, hydrangeas, and lilacs. In any case, start with young plants, preferably whips, that reach just to the base of a trellis.

The trellis may be of heavy wood or heavy wire or of metal piping, although metal is not the best selection for a hot climate. Place the trellis so it stands free of the wall with at least 6 inches of air-space behind it. Plants grown close to a wall often fail. English and German gardeners prefer a trellis that duplicates the desired pattern of a plant; French horticulturists tend to use a grid of lath or wire.

Prune your espalier-trained plants twice a year, and pinch them back throughout the growing season. After leaves fall in late autumn, cut back every lateral branch to two or three buds. If several laterals have developed close together, remove some to prevent a bunchy look. At the same time, shorten every terminal shoot. If growth has been desirably moderate, just cut back the tip to a promising side bud. If growth has been fairly extensive, remove up to two-thirds of the shoot, and consider a little root-pruning to retard growth.

With fruit trees, short stubby rough twigs, called "spurs," appear along the branches. These spurs bear flowers and, with luck, fruit. Protect them at all costs. But don't let them develop too close together; 5 or 6 inches is good spacing. When very old spurs branch repeatedly, either prune the spur or plan to thin out the fruit in early summer. Pruning spurs is risky business because spur wood is fragile; pruning also reduces the number of attractive spring flowers. Thinning the fruit is better policy.

Early in summer, pinch back each lateral branch as soon as it has made three or four leaves. This is important. It not only preserves the form of the plant, but also limits the food available for growth by reducing the photosynthetic surface of the plant. This is the carbohydrate or food-making area. Also pinch back terminal shoots when they have made a few inches of growth. As summer progresses, if too much leafy growth occurs, nip it out entirely.

When an espalier-trained tree persists in producing long, whippy shoots with large, soft foliage, the stern measure of root-pruning is called for. This is the only means of slowing down a too vigorous plant. Early in spring you can dig up and remove up to a third of the largest roots, cutting just below the crown. Then reset the plant. Root-prune older plants by trenching, as discussed in Chapter 2.

Prune evergreen espalier-trained trees and shrubs throughout the growing season. Start early in spring just before growth begins and work them over thoroughly. Remove crowding branches entirely; check terminal shoots to within a few inches of the previous year's wood; balance the volume of each arm against its counterpart by getting rid of enough twigs and leaves to achieve symmetry. With flowering shrubs, like pyracantha, vigorous trimming is also necessary in early spring. Too often pyracantha on a wall is left to form a solid green panel with no trace of ornamental pattern showing. Try to trim these leafy, flowering shrubs so as to reveal flowers and fruits.

Cordons, almost always grown from dwarf fruit trees, are two-dimensional, geometrically trained, but free-standing woody plants. While young, they are usually supported by wires, much like a grape support. Seldom seen in the United States, cordons are much used in Europe as garden ornaments or for commercial fruit production. Cordons are pruned the same way as espalier-trained plants.

Topiaries

Shearing woody plants into fanciful shapes is an ancient garden art. The early Romans practiced it. Through the Middle Ages and especially during the late Renaissance, topiaries were popular. The hours of careful manipulation required by topiary work have almost removed it from the modern gardening scene, except in Disneyland! However, some fine examples can still be seen in colonial gardens

THE FINE ART OF ESPALIER-TRAINING. Apple trees, set in a close row against a wall, are trained to a Y-shape, the branches secured to a lath lattice supported by heavy, galvanized wires. New shoots are now ready to be pinched back to one or two leaves. *Roche photo*

TOPIARY FEATURE. For this formal garden in Colonial Williamsburg, Virginia, a beautiful piece of topiary work in boxwood is centered in the axis of the walks. Such a tree is pruned every few weeks—a hedge shears is the proper tool in this case—to keep the rigid outlines from being blurred with new growth. *Molly Adams photo*

that exist in this country, as at Williamsburg, Virginia, and also in old English and European gardens.

Topiary trimming is begun when a plant is quite small. A scaffold of branches is slowly built up. Only twiggy species are suitable, such as boxwood, yew, rosemary (but only in mild climates), and privet. In tropical areas, Portuguese laurel is a possibility.

To develop properly, topiary specimens must be in an open exposure with full light on all sides. Shear them closely to build up a much-branched internal structure with a surface layer of dense, twiggy branchlets. A plant may be sheared into a column, then the top allowed to bulge gradually and a bear's head sculptured there with pruning shears. Two more excrescences of growth may become forelegs, the lowest portion of the plant sheared into haunches.

Topiary work amounts to horticultural sculpture. It is done in slow motion as the material being shaped increases in size. Tight shearing is required at least every few weeks and, at the height of the growing season, weekly shearing may be necessary to keep a vigorous specimen neat and trim. The amateur gardener may be gratified to know that every time he shears his Woodward globe arborvitae into a tight sphere, he is practicing topiary work just as surely as the skilled plantsman who maintains the magnificent seventeenth-century topiary collection at Levens Hall in England. At Compton Wynyates and Packwood, there are other fine English topiary gardens.

Miniature trees and bonsai

Dwarf trees are in vogue again. There are two methods of developing a dwarf tree. True dwarf forms of large trees occur in nature from time to time. These are avidly swept into collectors' gardens and propagated by grafting. Such dwarf specimens require no special trimming to insure their miniature size, only maintenance pruning, which consists of balancing the growth and occasionally thinning out the top. Usually these natural dwarfs are planted in rock gardens where they give scale to a stony landscape. The extensive and beautifully displayed Gotelli Collection of dwarf trees in the National

WHAT WILL THEY THINK OF NEXT! The ancient art of topiary has been revived in a new, exciting form at Disneyland where experts grow plants, mostly junipers, in containers and prune them into the forms of famous Disney characters and fanciful animals. It takes four years or more to create a perfect form like this elephant, which, as it is container grown, can be expected to last for some fifteen years. *Walt Disney Productions photo*

Arboretum at Washington, D. C., is open to the public throughout the year and offers a fine example of a well-maintained planting of these dwarf trees.

Centuries ago Chinese horticulturists developed fantastic stone landscape gardens. In them they planted young trees and, by continual pinching, weighting, and manipulating, they grew these into miniature duplicates of the wind-tossed, mountain-crag specimens they saw around them. Their technique was carried to Japan where the plants were grown in containers. Today we call trees grown this way "bonsai plants." To the Japanese, a natural miniature tree grown in a container is merely a "potted tree"; but a container-grown tree that has been artfully dwarfed by special culture and pruned is a "bonsai tree." Literally, bonsai means "grown in a container."

A cult has arisen around bonsai culture with directions for handling roots, killing cambium by bruising preselected areas, dissecting buds, and so on. Actually, the Japanese techniques are orderly and scientific. A catalogue of shapes determines the patterns. Specific soil mixtures, carefully blended and built up in the container through a series of intermingled layers, are recommended for each species, and procedures are set for shaping branches and trunks by wiring and weighting. Such involved techniques are beyond the scope of this book but a few suggestions are in order on pruning these artificially dwarfed, container-grown plants.

Generally speaking, young plants—including seedlings, layers, and rooted cuttings—are pruned rather severely. Being young, they contain a high proportion of embryonic or unspecialized tissues and these are capable of restoring any heavily pruned areas. Bonsai experts, working with a young plant and having confidence in its ability to survive, frequently remove a large part of the top and as much as half or more of the root system. Confidence is based not only on the known tolerance of a plant but also on the ability of the expert to regulate environmental conditions so that they will be favorable.

Older evergreen specimens—junipers, spruces, cryptomerias, and pines—cannot endure drastic pruning. In repotting, take great care to avoid root damage to any mature needled trees; the older they are, the more risky your task. If tops are to be reshaped, do this by wiring and weighting, never by drastic pruning. Older specimens make almost no new growth but if what does develop seems disproportionate, pinch it out as soon as it forms.

On the other hand, mature deciduous trees—elms, maples, hackberries, and particularly fruit trees—may be severely pruned but feed them rather heavily about thirty days beforehand. Then take great care to whittle away stubs and to finish off with a wood-working gouge that makes a clean, slightly concave surface where a branch has been removed. Thus, as the cambium restores itself, it grows over the scar and no wound is evident.

After young and old deciduous bonsai specimens have leafed out, it is a common practice in late spring or early summer to remove the leaves, forcing the development of a second crop of foliage that will be smaller and in better scale. If your plant does not thrive, with a small scissors cut away all the leaf blade except for a small, fan-shaped portion at the end of the petiole or leaf stem. When new leaves appear, completely remove these old, trimmed leaves. During the period of releafing, plants are in a precarious state and require most careful attention to culture.

LIVING SCULPTURE. The twisted trunks of this old flowering crabapple make the tree an effective garden feature, particularly in the winter landscape. Low stubs indicate where undesirable branches have been removed to clean the central scaffold. No suckers are allowed to clutter the strong sculptured form. *Miner photo*

Never trim the foliage of evergreens. Remove only the tender, new leafy shoots, partially or almost entirely as necessary. Do this with fine tweezers and a tiny knife just before the new growth hardens off. Always leave a few needles on the base of a shoot. When an evergreen branch reaches a desired length, you can retard growth by removing terminal buds with tweezers. Do it just before growth is resumed early in the season. Then foreshorten lateral growth substantially so as to create a pleasing form.

Here then are a few cardinal rules for bonsai:

Do not prune a completely dormant, dwarfed potted tree; if you do, chances are it will never wake up. Wait until growth has started.

Prune mature wood in several steps making the first cut with shears; immediately follow up with a sharp knife, whittling the stub flush, and finishing with a gouge to achieve a clean, concave surface.

Always prune just above a bud, and slant the cut away from the bud, as in other pruning procedures.

In summer, pinch to restrict growth; this is worth ten years of heavy pruning, particularly for the fragile miniatures.

Every few days through the growing season, work over your bonsai specimens, pinching out tips and brushing off buds that appear where branches are not wanted. Generally maintain the configuration of your plant and enhance it by manipulation of tender, young tissues.

For dramatic effect

A deciduous tree like a maple, particularly if it has not been regularly pruned when young, may have developed an arresting structure. By removing all but perhaps three great limbs and clearing these high of side growth, you can produce a dramatic specimen that will make a notable accent for your garden. A gnarled evergreen that at first appears to be only a shapeless mass can be made ornamental in much the same way. Just thinning out to reveal basic structure on a thickened crabapple can make it a far more interesting specimen that casts open shadows on the lawn instead of heavy shade.

Then there is the see-through value of trees to be considered. Thick growth around porches and terraces gives a shut-in feeling. Prune trees or big shrubs open so air and light comes through and you can enjoy vistas of your garden through the leaves. In the A to Z section, other suggestions are given for pruning to reveal some special beauty of bark or branch formation.

A to Z of Pruning Plants

Species or secondary names are given only when pruning directions are not generally applicable to the genus as a whole. Names in parenthesis on headings are common names that are hardly acceptable and the subject of much confusion. Insofar as possible, botanical nomenclature follows *Hortus Second* by L. H. Bailey and Ethel Zoe Bailey, and common names are in the style recommended by the Garden Writers of America Association.

PRUNING TO CONTROL SIZE AND SHAPE. Figures 1 and 2 show a typical side branch on a deciduous woody shrub as a forsythia. By cutting back shoots at A in Figure 1, buds can be forced, as shown in Figure 2. Such pruning thickens up a straggly plant, and, if done at the end of a branch, retards the spread. Figure 3 shows a too dense deciduous shrub pruned the right way—old wood thinned out some to the base. In Figure 4, more old wood is drop-pruned to a crotch. In Figure 5 an ornamental shrub is ruined by a flat-top trim; always try to preserve the natural shape of a plant. Figures 6 and 7 show how weak inner canes are cut to the ground; branches growing toward the center, removed; other branches headed back; the result a balanced amount of wood distributed within the body of the shrub. All cuts are made where branches originate or at a bud, as in Figure 1.

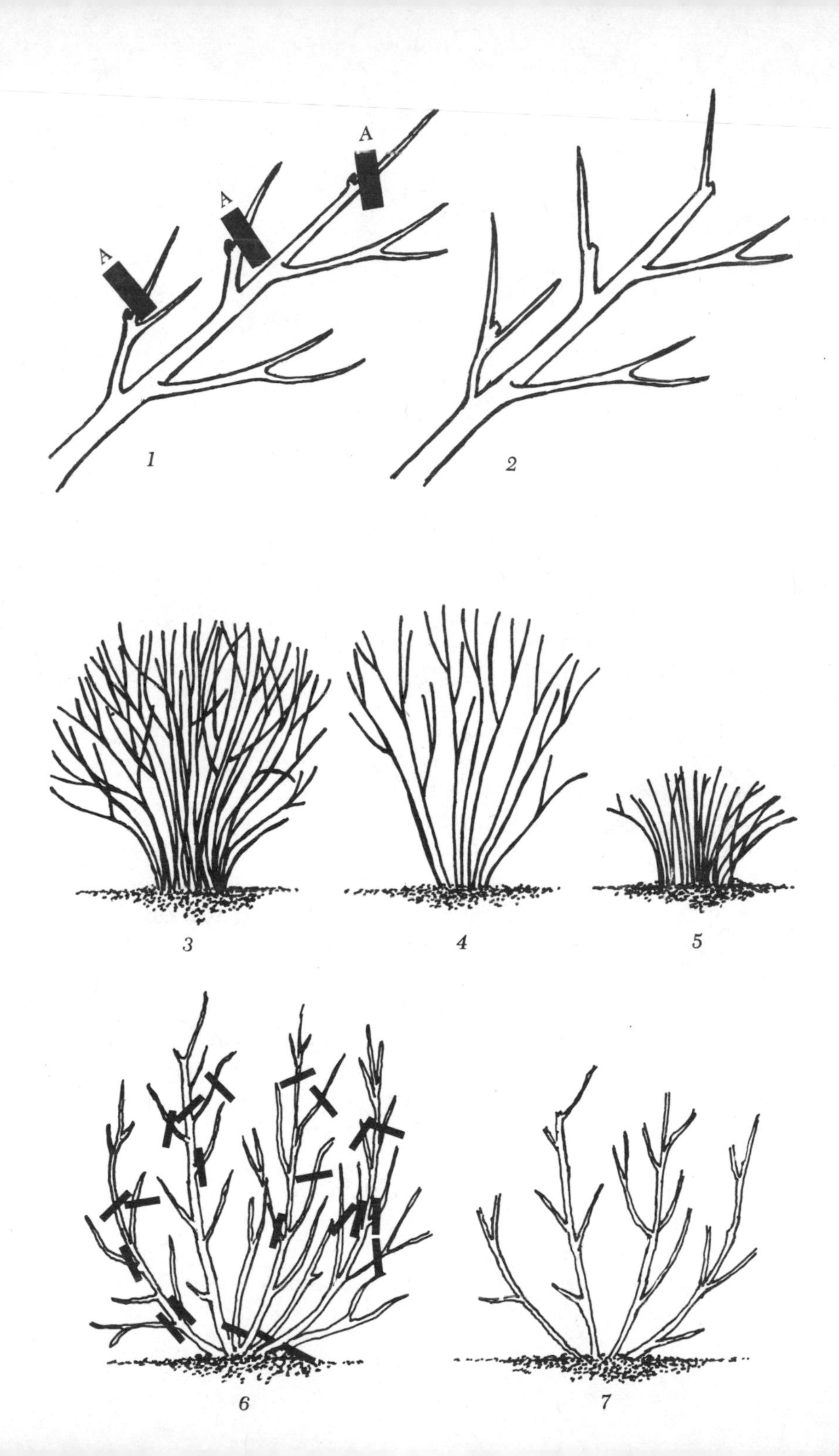
A
A
A
1
2
3
4
5
6
7

Abele see **POPULUS**

ABELIA grandiflora BUSH-ARBUTUS SPRING

This shrub suffers considerable damage in severe winters. As buds break, prune out dead twigs and whole branches that are slow in budding (probably from cambium damage). Every second or third year, remove a few of the oldest canes to the crown to stimulate new growth. When cutting for the house, take care not to destroy the graceful drooping habit. For the first two or three years in cold areas, where this is slow to establish, cut back old wood to the ground each spring after new basal shoots appear. Then pour a solution of potassium sulphate—½ cup to 3 gallons of water—around base of each plant in September. This helps to harden off immature wood. In tropical climates, remove old wood from tender species more frequently and constantly pinch back new basal shoots to induce low branching.

ABELIOPHYLLUM distichum WHITE-FORSYTHIA SPRING

Renovate after it blooms by cutting the oldest canes to the ground every third or fourth spring. Yearly pruning is not required. Frequently specimens of this open, upright-spreading shrub are ruined by tight trimming in an effort to force dense growth.

ABIES FIR WINTER

An old German text on horticulture has this to say about pruning fir trees [in translation] "the fir tree that requires pruning is mislocated and ought to be moved; if the specimen is valuable [it is] better to clear away surrounding plants and buildings." This tells the story! Fir trees should not be pruned except to remove injured or diseased branches. Wait for very cold weather and use pruners or a sharp saw. A copious flow of resinuous sap seals the wound. To retard growth of an entire limb, very early in spring remove the tip bud and all other buds for a foot or so below the tip. To fill in a thin area, remove terminal buds only from branches surrounding the gap. A burst of lateral twig growth will fill up the void. You may further limit growth of an overgrown limb by removing the terminal bud. Since this stimulates growth below on the limb, the same pinching out will fill out a sparse limb.

ABUTILON FLOWERING MAPLE CONTINUOUS

These tender mild-climate shrubs bloom on new wood. Where plants are evergreen, remove about a fourth of the branches every three months, cutting them way back inside the shrub; in this way you will renew the whole plant in a year's time and keep a vigorous crop of blooming wood coming on. Where cold weather drives the plants to dormancy (they cannot endure a freezing climate), stub them back to 8 inches and mound them with compost. When mild weather returns, recut to unstained wood, feed, and remove the weakest shoots as soon as growth reaches 12 inches. If your shrub is frosted, cut it back immediately and protect it until the weather warms up. Then recut it almost to the ground, for wood that shows any sign of injury will decay and damage the entire plant.

Acacia see **ALBIZZIA**

ACANTHOPANAX FIVE-LEAF ARALIA SPRING

This is the commonly encountered member of the genus; it tolerates shade and even thrives in the polluted air of cities. Where space permits, that is, for a 7- to 8-foot spread, let it develop a great billowy mass. Occasionally remove the oldest wood which you can identify by its zigzag conformation. Don't pinch or prune new shoots or unattractive broomy growth will develop. Where space is limited, cut to the ground each spring to produce a vertical shrub well furnished with handsome leaves. Since flowers are insignificant and fruit is seldom produced, nothing is lost by such harsh pruning.

ACER in variety MAPLE MID- OR LATE SUMMER

Pruning depends on type, use, and size. There are large, shade-tree maples, as sugar, Norway, and sycamore; smaller ornamentals, as trident and tatarian; the still smaller, often multiple-stemmed Amur; vine and mountain maples are often grown and pruned like large shrubs; the Japanese require special treatment because of unusual habit. Prune in mid- or late summer; winter and early spring pruning cause considerable bleeding. Seal off even small cuts with tree-wound dressing since maples are prone to decay caused by micro-organisms that enter through cuts.

Prune young shade-tree maples to one leader. Cut off about a third of the annual growth of side branches until the trunk reaches a 2-inch diameter. This practice builds a high sturdy crown and a tight branching system that will be carried on through the years. Because maple bark is thin and burns easily in winter, removing lower branches to achieve a clean trunk may result in sunscald. To avoid this, protect young, newly pruned or transplanted maples for three years or longer with tree-wrap.

Older maples require little pruning for they grow slowly, forming a billowy, symmetrical head. In the home garden, you can thin tops by drop-pruning (Chapter 2) to let in more light and raise the top or crown by removing lower branches so that other plants will have a chance to grow beneath the trees.

Let the ornamental *A. tataricum, A. griseum,* the paper-bark, *A. Buergerianum,* the trident maple, and *A. pensylvanicum* or moosewood develop as informal, graceful, small trees, with one or several trunks. Remove low branches only enough for easy mowing and display of the handsome bark formation. For a picturesque effect, you may want to get rid of some lateral branches.

Prune and train the small maples as large attractive shrubs—the

Amur, *A. Ginnala;* vine, *A. circinatum,* and mountain, *A. spicatum.* Let these beauties grow with three or more trunks, the lowest branches removed for a few feet, then thinned for a few feet. Pinch out and train tops in horizontal planes. With these shrubby maples, avoid removal of trunks at the ground line since they are not given to basal sprouting. In fact, consider well before removing any lower limb since it will not be replaced.

Prune the maples from Japan in Japanese style. Beside the familiar *A. palmatum* with its many varieties and cultivars, there is the full-moon maple, *A. japonicum,* of similar habit but with a broad leaf, and the somewhat larger species, as *A. diabolicum, A. nikoense,* and *A. argutum.* Use your judgment with these. First take a good look at your tree as it is; next visualize the basic trunk and limb structure as if the tree were ancient and wind-tossed on a mountain crag. Then prune accordingly. Make the most of the graceful tendency of these Oriental species to develop horizontal layers of tight, undulating growth. Space branches so that the gnarled trunk and limbs will show. There is no formula for pruning Oriental maples. Study pictures of them and visit an arboretum where they are well grown. Then trial-and-error pruning will show you the way.

Some maples require more pruning than any of these others, particularly the rapid-growing soft or silver maple, *A. saccharinum,* and the succulent box-elder, *A. nigundo.* Both overgrow with brittle wood that splits off in wind storms. A Midwestern error, particularly with silver maple, is to lop off the whole top, leaving great stark stubs sticking toward the sky. From these stubs grow broomy clusters of water sprouts, and decay soon sets in at the stub. But every two or three years these soft maples and large-elders do require top *thinning.* Remove selected branches at a crotch by drop-pruning (Chapter 2). The purpose is to lighten the twig and leaf burden equally over the crown of the tree while maintaining its natural form and symmetry. An expert may remove as much as half of the crown (a high proportion for this type of pruning), yet you will notice almost no change in your tree other than a somewhat less dense appearance. When you prune soft maples and box-elders, you may have to repaint cuts at least once to keep them sealed.

Hedge maple, *A. campestre,* is another special case. Eventually reaching 20 feet or more, it develops a compact, twiggy ball. It is best grown as a lawn specimen—untrimmed except for the removal of any injured wood—or for a high, dense, deciduous hedge. Then shear it tight.

ACTINIDIA CHINESE, TARA-, SILVER-VINE SUMMER-WINTER

These vines may be tender, as *A. chinensis,* Chinese actinidia, or hardy through Zone 4, as *A. arguta,* the Tara-vine, and *A. polygama,* the silver-vine. Except for *A. polygama,* they twine vigorously and grow several feet, even yards in one season. Through the summer thin out and train the long shoots that develop. (All vines grow best in one layer so keep this in mind when you prune.) Cut shoots back to side buds that face an open area of the trellis or remove some shoots entirely. In February, or later when buds begin to swell, remove old twiggy branches, dead wood, and superfluous shoots. Do most of the heavy pruning while vines are dormant. The fragile silver-vine requires little pruning. Protect it from cats; they will climb walls, even burgle a greenhouse to get at it, then claw and chew it to shreds. Only the male vine bears the handsome white-and-variegated new leaves.

AESCULUS HORSE-CHESTNUT, BUCKEYE LATE WINTER-EARLY SPRING

Prune tree and shrub forms in late winter or very early spring before sap flows. Remove crowded branches and head-back too vigorous new shoots. Prune young trees to insure a single leader; weak crotches are common because a terminal bud is frequently lost and the two lateral buds below form equal branches. Cut back one of these to an outward-facing twig; the unpruned side of the crotch will then dominate. Peg down the horizontal branches of the red buckeye, *A. pavia humilis,* an almost prostrate form used as intermediary between large shrubs and lawn. Remove strong upright shoots as they appear. In the Midwest the bottlebrush buckeye, grown as a ground-cover under large old trees, is pruned the same way.

AILANTHUS TREE-OF-HEAVEN WINTER

This is weedy and rapid-growing with sexes separate. The fruit of the male trees is foul-smelling when bruised and female trees clutter a neighborhood with progeny. Limit use to city plantings or cool, damp climates where growth is slower. You can get a tropical effect by planting several young trees in the same hole; remove all side branches as they appear, leaving only a crown of large, spreading leaves. For a shade tree, prune back side branches one-third to encourage the leader; thin the top frequently to strengthen the brittle, weak wood.

AKEBIA FIVE-LEAF AKEBIA WINTER-SPRING

Both *A. quinta* and *A. trifoliata* survive into Zone 5; they are evergreen in the South, deciduous in the North. Both grow rapidly, forming unmanageable tangles if allowed to encroach into a shrub border. Grow on a water downspout or other isolated vertical support where the vine can show off handsome foliage without becoming a problem. In winter, remove old wood on old plants. Since the vines twine, cut out inner canes a little at a time. Every ten years or so in spring, cut to the ground. In summer, regularly remove all dangling trailers and bushy side shoots. For easier maintenance try to limit a plant to two or three main trunks.

ALBIZZIA JAPANESE SILKTREE (ACACIA, MIMOSA) LATE SPRING

To avoid a lot of pruning in the North where young trees are liable to frost damage, pad trunks through winter with straw or excelsior and wrap with aluminum foil. If a young tree is winter killed, cut it to the ground. New sprouts will appear in early summer and these will require protection through winter. The next spring, remove all but one or three stems to develop either a one-trunk tree or a clump. With older trees that show fungus brackets and patches of dead bark (identified as sunken and yellowish), prune out branches and trunks. Make clean, vertical cuts and seal carefully because this tree does not heal well. In the South, where is grows into a great, high-crowned specimen, it needs a little drop-pruning (Chapter 2) every five years to lighten the top. In the North, it almost always stays low and spreading, often multiple-trunked with a shallow crown. Wait to prune until buds begin to break; then you can cut out all winter-injured and weak wood.

Alder see **ALNUS**

ALNUS ALDER LATE WINTER

Know which alder you are growing so you can prune according to natural form. Italian alder, *A. cordata,* is globe-shaped; Manchurian alder, *A. hirsuta,* and Japanese alder, *A. japonica,* are pyramidal.

White alder, A. *rhombifolia,* native to California, is a large tree with a high crown (trim this to feature the silvery bark but let some branches droop to show the handsome leaves, chartreuse below, deep green above). Growing as a shrub in the North and in dry areas, A. *incana,* the speckled alder, is a small tree in mild climates and in moist meadows; only the weeping form is attractive. Hazel alder, A. *rugosa,* also grows as a large shrub. Prune shrub forms for continual renewal at the base by cutting out one-third of the old canes every winter. At the same time, cut out the weakest new canes and shorten a few of the remaining canes by cutting to an outward-facing bud. Prune tree forms to a dominant leader by reducing the uppermost lateral branches by a quarter. Remove any side branches that turn upward except in pyramidal forms. Cut very old, unkempt alder shrubs to the ground and fertilize heavily to rejuvenate them. Pinch out some new shoots as they appear to encourage low branching.

Althea see **HIBISCUS**

AMELANCHIER SHADBLOW, SARVISBERRY WINTER

Remove basal suckers from tree forms—A. *laevis,* A. *canadensis,* and A. *arborea*—while they are young; protect the leader by shortening any side branches that tend to compete. Cut out crossing and crowding branches where they originate. Though wood heals rapidly, dress wounds to protect the easily decaying wood. Bushy types, often called shadbush, include A. *oblongifolia,* A. *prunifolia,* and A. *ovalis.* Remove the oldest wood from these every five or six years and pinch back the vigorous, unbranched shoots that appear the next growing season. There is no point in thinning the twiggy growth of some of these bush forms because blossoms are then lost; anyway shrubs belong in a woodsy setting where they can grow naturally. Spreading into sizable patches from well-rooted underground stems, A. *stolonifera* and A. *humilis* may be controlled by occasional severing of underground runners with a sharp spade. Remove crowding canes, very old canes, and canes that spread beyond the desired limit of your planting.

AMORPHA LEADPLANT, FALSE-INDIGO SUMMER–WINTER

Control the native indigo-bush, A. *fruticosa,* by pinching out new shoots in summer; remove any unsightly old canes at the ground line while plants are dormant. Do not shorten old canes or they will produce a cluster of broomy shoots just below the cut while the lower part of the old stalk thickens. This shrub should be allowed its natural height of 20 feet. Good conditions—a well-drained, gravelly, sunny spot—alleviates the need for pruning the beautiful, low-growing native leadplant, *A. canescens.* Just nip off spent flowers. For best effect in the perennial bed, this one may be cut to the ground occasionally, or even annually. All amorphas sucker when they thrive; use a sharp spade to remove unwanted sprouts or pull them up after rain when the ground is soft.

AMPELOPSIS MONKSHOOD-, HOP-, PEPPER-VINE

WINTER–EARLY SPRING

Pruning varies according to type so study the growth habit of your vine. (Nomenclature is too confused to be helpful.) In early spring, prune the hardy kind. It has crisp, airy foliage that looks fragile, being deeply divided, but is really durable. Remove crisscross growth, knobby old wood, and shoots that grow out from the base toward nearby shrubs. You may even cut it to the ground for complete renewal. Prune while dormant the porcelain ampelopsis, *A. brevipedunculata,* with berries that shade from green to rose, then turn delft blue. This tendril climber is hardy through Zone 4. Remove "nests" of branching, spur-bearing old wood by cutting to a clean branch; head back young, stringy, unbranched vines by cutting to a bud. Remove any tendrils that fail to find a climbing surface. Through the summer, prune off whippy, unattached young shoots dangling away from the main vine.

The two tender species demand steady attention. Pepper-vine, *A. arborea,* is rampant; through summer, cut away all shoots that develop beyond desirable bounds. Pull or dig out suckers in lawn or borders; if they are 10 feet or more from the parent plant, cut them off flush with the ground and paint the stump with an oil solution of weed-killer —2, 4-D or 2, 4, 5-T brush-killer. The underground shoot will die back a ways without harming the parent plant. Hop ampelopsis, *A. humulifolia,* tends to be shrubby; thin it several times through the growing season and remove branches that grow out from the support. It is evergreen in the South, deciduous at the northern limit of its range.

Andromeda see **PIERIS**

Angelica-tree see **ARALIA**
Antarctic-beech see **NOTHOFAGUS**

ANTIGONON CORAL-VINE CONTINUOUS

This tender vine climbs to 40 feet or more and, unless kept spread to a single layer, may form a thick mass of living and dead stems entwined in a hopeless tangle. Grow it on a wire trellis, head-back the main vines as needed, and remove some of the branches as the body of the plant becomes too massive. From time to time, cut one or two of the oldest stems to the ground—a job, this, as it must be disentangled from the supports. Allow a new shoot to take its place. If spent flower-heads are not removed, you may find a crop of seedlings throughout the garden. Birds find the seeds much to their liking.

Apple see **MALUS**
Apricot see **PRUNUS**

ARALIA DEVIL'S-WALKING-STICK, HERCULES-CLUB, ANGELICA-TREE MID-SPRING

For tree-form (difficult), prune to a single stem; if grown as a well-spaced clump of three or more, prune to keep trunks clean of foliage. Save enough of the freely produced suckers to replace diseased or spent shoots; cut out the rest with a sharp spade. Even so, these coarse, prickly shrubs cannot be controlled and are best planted where a neat appearance is not required. The rather tender Japanese angelica-tree, *A. elata,* growing to 40 feet is the most refined species; *A. chinensis* is shorter, seldom exceeding 20 feet, and is intermediate in coarseness between *A. elata* and the native *A. spinosa.* This form with prickles on the great, bipinnate leaves is useful for pseudo-tropical or "gravel and boulder" plantings where, pruned to single stems with no branches, it looks like a palm tree.

ARAUCARIA MONKEY-PUZZLE TREE, NORFOLK ISLAND-PINE EARLY SPRING

The commonest outdoor species, monkey-puzzle tree, *A. araucana,* is one of a group of ancient conifers, its tissues and bud behavior not comparable to any familiar garden tree. It resents pruning, but new growth may be shortened as it appears. Don't interfere with the leader and don't cut back old wood or the tree will develop a "flat-chested" look on the cut side. Cut off old lower limbs (for clearance) at the trunk and seal the wounds. Norfolk Island-pine, *A. excelsa,* the popular Victorian parlor ornament, can be kept in bounds by pinching back soft new growth uniformly over the plant. Or just before repotting in early spring, remove about a third of the leader and half of all recent growth on lateral branches.

Arborvitae see **THUJA**

ARBUTUS MADRONA, STRAWBERRY-TREE MIDWINTER

If you grow madrona, *A. menziesii,* as a specimen, remove enough branches to feature the gnarled zigzag growth of the crown and the handsome trunk. If it is multiple-trunked, perhaps as a dooryard specimen, pinch back new growth to force early development of contorted branching. The strawberry-tree, *A. unedo,* may be grown as a large bush, as a small, rather formal tree, or trimmed to form a globed standard. Remove long, vigorous shoots breaking out on the lower limbs of shrubs and trees and, when the tree is dormant, thin out just enough old growth to feature the handsome fruits. Shear standards throughout the growing season to keep tops tight and even. (This is not the trailing arbutus, *Epigaea repens,* the Mayflower of northeastern woods.)

ARCTOSTAPHYLOS MANZANITA, BEARBERRY, KINNIKINNICK WINTER–SPRING

Prune shrubby types to feature the beautiful reddish branches and interesting growth habit. Retain only three or four trunks to a plant and thin branches to keep bushes open. If, following severe pruning, a heavy crop of buds appears low on the trunks, rub them off before they become shoots. To preserve old plants, occasionally cut off a very old trunk right at the ground level. Specimens pruned to form small, multiple-trunked trees require almost no pruning once they develop satisfactory form. When they spread too far, clip back newly planted, ground-cover bearberry clumps (kinnikinnick) severely just before spring growth begins. Prune off all shoots that stick up through the smooth green blanket.

ARISTOLOCHIA DUTCHMAN'S-PIPE SPRING–FALL

Train rather than prune these vines. Both A. *durior* and A. *tomentosa,* hardy into Zone 5, make excellent, almost carefree screens if heavy foliaged vines are spread out on trellis or latticework as they develop. At any time, remove pieces that twine about each other, trim off dangling sections, and thin out the basal shoots that break in spring. After a severe winter, remove all slow-to-break and dead wood as soon as buds swell on live wood. To rejuvenate old vines, fertilize heavily for a year beforehand; then cut to the ground in early spring. Cut herbaceous species, as A. *serpentaria,* the native Virginia snakeroot, to the ground in late fall. Prune greenhouse-grown tropical and tender kinds as they renew their growth in March. Thin out the mature vines, head-back overgrown ones, and, if they show no flower buds, cut off tag-ends that fall away from supports.

ARONIA CHOKEBERRY WINTER–MIDSUMMER

When black chokeberry, A. *melanocarpa,* stands in front of high plantings, drop-prune tops back about a third (Chapter 2) and remove a few of the oldest branches every third or fourth year. Spade out the freely produced suckers that appear beyond bounds. In a woodland setting, prune as little as possible. Tall growing red chokeberry, A. *arbutifolia,* and the purple-fruited A. *prunifolia* are best grown with several well-spaced trunks. Head-back vigorous terminal shoots produced after flowering, and pinch lateral shoots throughout the growing season. Very little pruning will give you a handsome shrub well furnished with foliage clear to the ground. When borers attack, cut out infested trunks and burn them; apply a systemic insecticide to protect what is left. If a shrub has required heavy pruning, feed generously and keep well watered; otherwise weak, spindly new shoots will grow back.

ARTEMISIA SOUTHERNWOOD, WORMWOOD, SAGEBRUSH SPRING

In the perennial border, remove spent blossoms from all types, head-back overgrown stalks, and cut the whole plant to the ground at the end of the growing season. The semiwoody Roman wormwood, A. *pontica,* and A. *frigida,* may be sheared into low, silvery hedges. Remove old wood frequently from tall-growing, shrubby types, as southernwood, A. *abrotanum,* and wormwood, A. *absinthium.* A good practice each spring is to cut out half of the stems at the crown; at the same time, correct the over-all form by nipping back straggly branches. Pinch new growth through the summer to get fuller, less leggy growth. Prune young specimens of native American sagebrush to one or three to five trunks. Don't remove any lower branches because they may not be replaced. Thin the branches on established plants to produce a weatherbeaten, gnarled effect. Sagebrush, grown with low silvery artemisias, makes a fine planting for arid banks where a minimum of pruning is desirable; just cut out stems contributing to a straggly, unkept look.

ARUNDINARIA CANE, BAMBOO SPRING–FALL

Remove old ragged canes at the crown so the canebrake does not look frowsy. Try to keep the patch within bounds by severing creeping underground stems as required. You will need a heavy spade or sharp axe to do the job. The native *A. gigantea* behaves well at first but forms an impenetrable thicket within ten years. Don't cut back the canes themselves or ill-proportioned broomy growth will result.

ARUNDO donax GIANT-REED FALL–WINTER

In the North, where it freezes back, cut this gigantic grass to the ground in fall. In the South, remove some of the old, branchy canes through the winter. If the heavy, subsurface stems spread out too rapidly, scrape away the soil and cut them back with a hatchet. If the ornamental variegated form throws an occasional all-green cane, cut it out with an adjoining piece of crown before it multiplies and green dominates the variegation. This plant with tall, thick, straight stems and wide, cornlike leaves in two ranks, bears a silvery plume in late summer, smaller than that of true pampas grass, with which, like cane and bamboo, it is often confused. Pruning methods are not the same.

Ash see **FRAXINUS**

ASIMINA triloba PAWPAW SPRING

In shady woodland this small tree needs little pruning, but you may have to dig out a few suckers from time to time or cut out dead wood from an old specimen. Prune specimen lawn trees to a single leader by cutting back side shoots near the top of the plant. Shorten all new growth on young plants to fill out the sparse branching.

Aspen see **POPULUS**

AUCUBA japonica JAPANESE AUCUBA SPRING–SUMMER
A specimen plant requires little pruning if you grow it where it is hardy and in light shade. At the northern limit of Washington, D.C., cut out winter-injured branches as soon as they are noticeable in spring. Pinch back too vigorous shoots when they reach out beyond the crown. Immediately cut out all-green color breaks on variegated forms—*A. japonica latimaculata* and *A. j. aureo-maculata*. Shear hedges two or three times through summer with a large, hand-operated hedge shears; the coarse leaves soon jam the blades of power pruners.

Avocado see **PERSEA americana**

AZALEA AZALEA (not honeysuckle) LATE SPRING–MIDSUMMER
It is important to know the growth form of these varied plants before you do much pruning. As a rule, the evergreen Japanese cultivars tend to be dense, low, and spreading but there are exceptions. The deciduous hybrids are upright, sparsely branched, and more difficult to shape; but, again, some are twiggy and some spread out. Many botanical species grow with one or just a few trunks but some of the evergreen ones, as *A. poukhanensis,* have a low, spreading, and self-layering habit. From all of them remove wilting flowers. In ten days or so new shoots will break out just below the spent flower-head. To keep plants in bounds and to develop more branches, clip these shoots back just as they harden. If you use hedge shears on Kurume types to make the work less tedious, take care not to prune them into green blobs; clip to natural contours.

Azaleas produce a crop of latent buds regardless of where branches are cut, so you are not bound to cut at a node (leaf joint) if another place seems better. You need to know this when trimming deciduous hybrids. Once they are established, vigorous Exbury, Knap Hill, de Rothschild, and Ghent types throw long, vigorous, unbranched canes from the crown. Early in summer pinch these back to various heights while they are still soft or cut them back as they harden. Watch for another crop of unbranched shoots in midsummer on both evergreen and deciduous kinds. Nip these back close to the ground to get more branches. On evergreen varieties, they usually arise from old

Figure 1

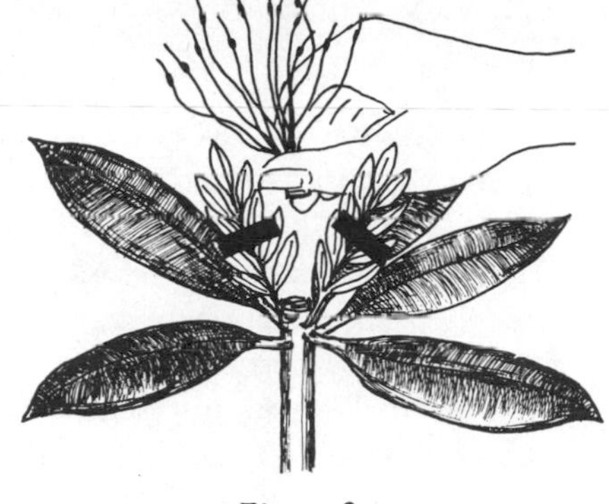

Figure 2

CONTROLLING GROWTH ON AZALEAS AND RHODODENDRONS. In Figure 1, the flower is fully opened. In Figure 2, the faded flower is removed; the new growth on each side is half formed. Now the plant will look tidy and not be weakened by seed formation. At the same time, new growth is pinched back to about half its length, or a little less, to keep the plant compact. For best results, do this while leaves are still small. With the tiny-leaved Oriental azaleas, you can use a clippers or hedge shears to cut over the plant but take care to preserve the natural contour.

wood below the bushy part of the plant. To renew old azaleas, fertilize them well for a year, then in spring remove at the ground half or more of the oldest canes. Pinch new shoots as they appear. Pinch out tips of rooted cuttings when you plant them and shear them for a year or two to make them bushy.

Bald-cypress see **TAXODIUM**
Bamboo see **ARUNDINARIA** or **PHYLLOSTACHYS**
Barberry see **BERBERIS**
Basswood see **TILIA**
Bayberry see **MYRICA**
Bead-tree see **MELIA**
Bearberry see **ARCTOSTAPYHLOS**
Beauty-berry see **CALLICARPA**
Beauty-bush see **KOLKWITZIA**
Beech see **FAGUS**
Benzoin see **LINDERA**

BERBERIS BARBERRY WINTER–SUMMER

Prune your hedge or specimen plants according to their normal growth form. The deciduous Japanese barberry, *B. Thunbergii*, grows broad and twiggy; wintergreen barberry, *B. Julianae*, grows upright and is less twiggy. Every second or third year, prune mature *deciduous* plants (grown as specimens) through the winter, removing a few of the oldest wood to let in air and light. On very old plants, thin out up to half of the mature wood. To feature the handsome fruit on some species, also thin the twiggy top growth through the winter. Some *evergreen* barberries develop a dense, crowded cluster of almost unbranched canes. Just before bud-break in spring, use a lopper to thin out weak and old canes, cutting them back to the crown. Through summer, pinch out new basal shoots while they are low. (If you wait to cut back the tall ripe canes next year, a cluster of branches will develop at the top and give the plant a broomy look.)

Set out plants for a hedge lower than they grew in the field and cut them back severely. For a few years, prune your hedge to an inverted V-shape. Then it will grow dense all the way to the ground. Later you can prune it to a flat top, but always cut a hedge with sloping sides and wider at the bottom than at the top.

BETULA BIRCH MIDSUMMER

Birches resent pruning and many mature trees are lost from decay or weakening due to bad pruning and over-pruning. You can grow a young tree to a single leader by nipping back the side branches near the top that threaten to dominate a clear-cut main stem. Remove lower limbs (if mowing requires it), before they are much more than half-an-inch thick. Never prune when the tree is bare or in early spring or your tree may bleed to death. Be careful of the thin bark on white birches and other smooth-bark forms. Once this is scarred or peeled off, it will be replaced by coarse, usually black, corky bark, and your lovely tree will be permanently marred.

BIGNONIA CROSS-VINE, TRUMPET-VINE (not trumpet-creeper) WINTER–SPRING–SUMMER

Just before buds break, prune the native *B. capreolata,* which is not to be confused with the rampant, orange-flowered trumpet-creeper, *Campsis radicans.* Remove all weak shoots, overgrown side branches, and strands that have fallen away from the support. Always cut to a joint as stubs are noticeable and apt to decay. Train to one layer. If you are trying this as a ground-cover, set the vines close and cut them back hard. Through summer pinch new growth; in winter, peg down year-old runners. Cut off all vertical shoots. When the cover is

STUDY OF TREE FORMS. This great white birch has been pruned high to open the view of flowering dogwoods whose lovely horizontal planes are becoming emphasized with age—and with judicious pruning. Just behind the trunk of the birch, appear the strongly ascending branches of a beech tree, while to the right the open, leafy top of a young wild cherry tree shows its well-spaced, open, branching habit. It is important to prune so as to enhance the natural shapes of your trees. *Miner photo*

established, continue to remove upright shoots and overlaying runners that choke out lower parts of the plant.

Big-tree see **SEQUOIA**
Birch see **BETULA**
Bittersweet see **CELASTRUS**
Black alder see **ILEX**
Blackberry see **RUBUS**
Black gum see **NYSSA**
Blackhaw see **VIBURNUM**
Bladder-nut see **STAPHYLEA**
Bladder-senna see **COLUTEA**
Bluebeard see **CARYOPTERIS**
Blueberry see **VACCINIUM**
Blue-spirea see **CARYOPTERIS**
Boston-ivy see **PARTHENOCISSUS**
Bottle-brush see **MELALEUCA linariifolia** or **CALLISTEMON**

BOUGAINVILLEA LATE WINTER

In the South, grow this woody vine as a wall plant on a trellis; in the North, as a conservatory plant. Cultivars are also grown as pot shrubs. Prune to develop a scaffold of woody trunks evenly spaced over a trellis. Prune back year-old lateral shoots in February to two buds. Either remove or stop-back at a bud long, unbranched basal suckers and too vigorous terminal shoots. If much of this sappy new growth remains on the plant, flowering will be reduced. Renew old vines by cutting to the ground. Strong, unbranched shoots will soon appear. Pinch these continuously to stimulate low branching and to slow down their growth. On potted plants, prune all new growth to two buds as it develops or remove it entirely if the plant is getting too dense. As blooming ends, cut out the twiggy growth that has borne flowers.

Boysenberries see **RUBUS**
Box, boxwood see **BUXUS**
Box-thorn see **LYCIUM**
Broom see **GENISTA**

BROUSSONETIA PAPER-MULBERRY WINTER

These tender ornamentals need little pruning. Remove weak and crowded limbs and small branches, cutting back to a crotch. If long, whippy sprouts grow through the crown from lower scaffold branches, remove them entirely as they start to grow or pinch them frequently to help fill out the top. Seal wounds as wood decays easily. Grow *B. papyrifera* as a small, rather craggy, picturesque tree; don't prune to formalize it. Prune *B. Kazinokii* as a large spreading shrub or as a standard similar to the umbrella catalpa. Either way, every winter remove the oldest canes to the base; thin out the rest, and head-back a few branches.

Buck-brush see **SYMPHORICARPOS**
Buckeye see **AESCULUS**
Buckthorn see **RHAMNUS**

BUDDLEIA SUMMER-LILAC, BUTTERFLY-BUSH SPRING–FALL

Prune according to type; some bloom on new wood, others on year-old or older branches. In spring, cut back to stubby crowns the *B. Davidii* group that blooms on new wood. This includes 'Black Knight', 'Empire Blue', 'Fascinating', 'Flaming Violet', 'Fortune', 'Peace', 'Purple Prince', 'White Profusion' and others. Finish all pruning before buds break in spring. *Do not cut these to the ground.* The ideal structure is a crown of well-spaced, 3- to 6-inch stumps, each with a knob of stubby, bud-bearing branches. Preserve this old wood. For a full, vigorous bush, cut back to within 2 to 3 inches of it each spring. As new growth develops, pull out all weak and crowded shoots. North of Zone 5, around Thanksgiving, it is necessary to lop back to about 15 inches. Then mound the crown with a porous mulch and cover with an inverted bushel basket. In spring, remove the covering and prune.

Prune those that bloom on old wood after they flower. These include mild-climate growers like *B. asiatica, B. Colvilei, B. globosa, B. officinalis,* and the hybrid, *B. Farquhari. Cut out at the ground* old twiggy branches that produce only undersized leaves. Limit other pruning to moderate thinning of internal growth and, perhaps gently head-back upright growers by cutting high new shoots to half their length. Renew old plants in this group by cutting them to the ground in early spring. A year's bloom must be sacrificed. Thin the new shoots as they appear and pinch them to encourage branching close to the ground.

B. alternifolia is a special case. Every three or four years remove a few of the oldest canes at the ground. Let it grow to its normal 10 feet and don't restrict spread or you will sacrifice the long, willowy, arching branches that bear the flowers.

To keep the head tight and globe-shaped on all standard forms, through summer repeatedly pinch out all tender growth.

Buffalo-berry see **SHEPHERDIA**
Bull-bay see **MAGNOLIA**

BUMELIA FALSE-BUCKTHORN, THUNDERWOOD WINTER

Prune in winter and paint wounds since these trees heal slowly. Limit pruning to removal of interfering branches and to thinning the head for a picturesque effect. False buckthorn, *B. lanuginosa,* exudes quantities of glassy clear, thick gum from wounds on large limbs and trunk. Thunderwood, *B. lycioides,* is almost identical but resents the heavy pruning that the false-buckthorn tolerates.

Burning-bush see **EUONYMUS**
Bush-arbutus see **ABELIA grandiflora**
Bush-clover see **LESPEDEZA**
Bush-honeysuckle see **DIERVILLA**
Butterfly-bush see **BUDDLEIA**
Butternut see **JUGLANS**
Button-bush see **CEPHALANTHUS**

BUXUS BOX, BOXWOOD SPRING–FALL

This tolerates any amount of pruning and also looks well unpruned when it forms great, dense, billowy bushes. Final shape and size depend on species. Pinch rooted cuttings several times before planting out; then shear tight for at least three years to develop density. Shear hedges and topiaries. In the North, before new growth appears, use your freshly sharpened hedge shears in spring to remove shoots produced late the previous summer; shear the new growth after it has begun to harden. In mild climates, shear hedges and topiary specimens in late fall so they will look attractive through winter. To control disease prune hard. For various reasons box may suddenly develop cankers and grow very twiggy, then entire branches die back. The minute you see that a patch of leaves has turned pale green, reach in and cut the branch back to healthy, dark green growth. Cut out every trace of wood that shows discoloration inside or that has sunken patches or blotches on the bark, and dip pruners in disinfectant between cuts; a solution of mercuric chloride (poisonous, from drug-store) 1:1000 is good or 70 percent alcohol.

Calamondin see **CITRUS**
California-lilac see **CEANOTHUS**

CALLICARPA BEAUTY-BERRY, FRENCH-MULBERRY WINTER–SPRING

Every winter remove old and crowded wood; keep none more than three or four years. Don't prune back stalks because this ruins appearance. Nip out interfering shoots, cutting back to the trunk from which they grow. North of Washington, D.C., the French-mulberry, *C. americana,* suffers injury. As the bush starts to bloom, cut out dead twigs with your smallest clippers. Allow the tall *C. bodinieri* and *C. dichotoma,* their full 10 feet. More suitable for home gardens is *C. japonica* growing to only about 4 feet.

CALLISTEMON BOTTLE-BRUSH CONTINUOUS

These tender shrubs thrive outside only in very mild climates. Drop-prune (Chapter 2) to open those that tend to become dense and brushy. When flowers fade, cut back vigorous shoots halfway and remove weak shoots entirely or, if they are needed to fill out a sparse plant, cut them back two-thirds and pinch the tips of new side shoots as they reach 6 inches. Most species grow very slowly; too often gardeners ignore them until severe pruning is required to bring them back to prime blooming condition. Do right by your bottle-brush and work it over at least once a year.

CALLUNA HEATHER EARLY SPRING

Adapt your pruning to your heather; if it is a yard-high type, cut back the previous year's growth enough to keep it dense and neat; if it is a prostrate, refined little fellow, leave it alone. Grow on well-drained, sandy, acid soil that is quite lean and you will never have to prune. If you plant in rich soil and feed, no amount of pruning will prevent straggly growth. With variegated forms—bronze, gold-leaved, and others—watch for all-green branches; cut these out as soon as they appear. If a plant develops long shoots that lay over, cut these out before they smother the branches below.

CALYCANTHUS CAROLINA ALLSPICE, SWEET-SHRUB SPRING

Prune when buds swell; remove weak and dead branches to the ground and clip out dead twigs; always cut to an outward-facing bud or back to a main trunk. In rich, moist, woodsy loam and partial shade, plants are thrifty and need little pruning; in the wrong location, considerable die-back must be pruned off every year.

CAMELLIA SUMMER

Remove blossoms as they fade. As new growth hardens, limit specimen plants by nipping back new shoots to two or three leaves. Clip out twigs that bear puny leaves or that show die-back; if scale, red spider, or other problems develop, thin out some branches so air and sprays can penetrate. Renewal of large, old plants is under study in several notable gardens. Although these shrubs do not take kindly to heavy pruning, removing one or two large trunks a year by cutting back to a low fork right after flowering seems to be promising. Heavy feeding brings on a crop of buds low on old wood.

CAMPSIS TRUMPET-CREEPER WINTER–SUMMER

The man faced with salvaging a fifty-year-old vine must take drastic measures for these rampant woody climbers can engulf a building or a large tree, wrapping around any available support and clinging with rootlike holdfasts. Cut such old, badly entwined vines to the ground; then select and train new shoots. With a spade, cut out root suckers that form around most vines, but especially old vines that have been severely pruned. To keep plants in hand, remove excess wood in winter, saving only a few main stalks, and shorten laterals on these. Head-back flowering shoots as blooms are shed in late summer. At any time, cut back overlong trailing tendrils to two or three leaves.

Candytuft see **IBERIS**
Cane see **ARUNDINARIA**
Cape-plumbago see **PLUMBAGO capensis**

CARISSA HEDGE-THORN, NATAL-PLUM, KARANDA SPRING–SUMMER

On young plants, shear back new growth after bloom. Older specimens slow down and may require no other pruning than the occasional removal of a branch that gets too long. Though plants are naturally dense, in hedges they require several shearings through the growing season to keep them neat. Of the three commonly grown in America, hedge-thorn, *C. Arduina*, and the Natal-plum, *C. grandiflora*, are best for hedging. *C. Carandas* is handsome as a specimen. Being tender, plants frequently die back in winter. When growth starts in spring, prune out dead and slow wood; if the plant is badly hurt by prolonged cold or ocean spray, cut it to the ground and hope for renewal.

Carolina allspice see **CALYCANTHUS**

CARYA HICKORY, PECAN SUMMER

Prune young garden trees to a single leader, shortening all side branches to half their length the season after they grow. As trees reach a diameter of 3 to 4 inches, remove a large proportion of the lateral limbs at the trunk. Remove lower limbs as the tree grows taller because the limbs will droop later and headroom will become a problem. With age most hickories develop a widespread, somewhat open crown and require little maintenance. Their only drawback for lawn use is the production of nuts, which attract swarms of squirrels and small boys. Young trees require two years of preparation before they can be moved; trench halfway round the roots one spring, and fill the trench with moist compost; next spring trench the other side and cut under the tree to sever roots growing straight down. Move the tree the third year and prune heavily to compensate for loss of roots.

Trees grown for nut production are pruned to a modified leader about the same as peach trees (see *Prunus*). Work for a much-branched, low crown by stopping the terminal shoot at elbow height; this will encourage the development of a scaffold of wide-crotched side branches. Head these back once or twice to develop a tight, round head. Remove in-growing and weak branches from older trees. Unpruned pecan trees make magnificent specimens, growing to 100 feet or more.

CARYOPTERIS BLUEBEARD, BLUE-SPIREA EARLY SPRING

Cut to the ground in the North where tops winter-kill; for a heavy flower crop, prune to short, bud-bearing stumps as for butterfly-bush (see *Buddleia Davidii*). Every spring in mild climates cut back about a third of the oldest canes at ground level, and thin out the twiggy growth, particularly toward the inside of the shrub. Never prune or pinch through the summer for this will reduce the fall crop of flowers.

CASTANEA CHESTNUT SUMMER

For a nut crop but not a lawn specimen, prune like a pecan (see *Carya*). Otherwise, prune for a leader, and that is a task because Chinese chestnuts, *C.mollissima* and their forms, tend to grow as low-branching, twiggy affairs with little beauty. If you can find a leader, remove all laterals that appear for a foot or more below its tip and heavily prune back all side branches below that point. Failing to find a leader, make one; select a branch that tends to grow more or less upright and is centered on the trunk. Remove all other large branches to the trunk and trim back the side branches of this "leader." Old trees need only normal maintenance.

CATALPA INDIAN-BEAN LATE SUMMER–WINTER

Prune according to natural form of species. The eastern *C. bignonioides,* is a moderately tall, very broad-spreading, round-headed tree; the western *C. speciosa* is vigorous, tall, and columnar; the hybrid of *C. bignonioides* and *C. ovata* has the broad eastern form but is smaller. Train young trees to a single leader by cutting off the less crooked side of any crotch that occurs along the main stem. Space side branches, saving those with the widest crotches. Older trees on the decline may be carried along for years by removing weak limbs, branches that fail to produce a full crop of normal leaves, and dead wood. Seal wounds to prevent decay.

Standards, called "umbrella catalpas," are made by grafting the dwarf form, *C. bignonioides nana,* to a straight stalk of any tall form at a 6- to 8-foot height. Cut back repeatedly the grafted shoot to develop a "hedgehog" or knob of short bud-producing stubs. Every winter cut back to the knob the long shoots of the previous year. The umbrella catalpa is marketed frequently as *C. Bungei* but this a different tree.

CEANOTHUS NEW-JERSEY-TEA, CALIFORNIA-LILAC EARLY SPRING
EARLY SUMMER

Remove faded flower-heads. Inland ceanothus, *C. ovatus,* and New-Jersey-tea, *C. americanus,* both hardy, require little other pruning than removal of one or two old stems over a three-year period. The tender and barely hardy shrubs in this genus range from prostrate plants to 30-foot giants. Most of them are grown as wall shrubs, fanned out for protection; in mild climates, you may grow them in the open garden. Prune wall-trained plants after flowering; reduce last year's bloom shoots to two or three buds; shorten all outward-growing branches to two or three leaves. Free-standing specimens require less severe pruning of young wood, but remove a few of the oldest canes each year. In early summer, prune spring-flowering varieties; in early spring, prune those that flower late summer and autumn.

Cedar see **CEDRUS.** (American "cedar" is **JUNIPERUS.**)

CEDRUS CEDAR (not juniper) SUMMER

True cedars have needles, not scales, and the needles grow in clusters on stubby side branchlets. Young cedars that are cone-shaped —including cedar of Lebanon (*C. libani*), Deodar cedar (*C. Deodara*), and Atlas cedar (*C. atlantica*)—require no pruning except to shorten disproportionate side branches. Very young cedars grow as indeterminate small bushes with no distinct leader; don't ruin these by trying to prune to a leader; in time one will develop, breaking away from the young growth. After two or three years, you can clip away some of the original "bush." The tendency to grow straight up in cone shape is lost when trees reach 50 feet or more. Then the crown spreads out rather like that of an old honey-locust. When this occurs, remove lower lateral branches at the trunk. On color forms, weeping forms, and other ornamental cedars in the garden, every year pinch back up to half of the new growth to keep plants small. (Illus., p. 84.)

CELASTRUS BITTERSWEET, WAXWORK EARLY SPRING–SUMMER

Early in spring, remove weak shoots and about a third of the newest wood, but adapt your pruning to the location of your vine. Grown in a wild garden where it can ramp freely over high shrubs or in the cultivated garden on a big pergola, this needs more training than pruning. On a trellis or fence—always against lath or wire on which it can twine—it requires heavy pruning. Cut the long, green, summer shoots halfway back unless they are well berried. Your vine may not fruit though it blooms; it usually needs a mate, since the

sexes are often separate. A planting of half a dozen vines is best for the native waxwork, *C. scandens.* With Korean bittersweet, *C. flagellaris,* and Oriental bittersweet, *C. orbiculatus,* you need only two or three vines to get a good crop of berries.

CELTIS HACKBERRY, SUGARBERRY SPRING–SUMMER–WINTER

In spring prune young trees to a single leader by cutting back soft, green side shoots all along the main stem to two or three leaves. Year-old and older side branches require no more pruning. Deciduous American species need almost no pruning. If they grow rapidly, evergreen Mediterranean types require December thinning every five or six years. In summer prune "witches brooms" out of young trees; there is nothing that really controls this condition which is caused by a mite that is followed by a fungus; and it is impossible to remove all the brooms from a mature tree.

CEPHALANTHUS BUTTON-BUSH WINTER

If you grow this at water's edge or in a damp ditch, it will need no pruning. To keep a large specimen planted elsewhere from outgrowing its location, every winter remove some of the oldest wood to the ground, taking care not to ruin the globular form. Don't try to maintain an open crown; it is natural for this plant to send up a dense cluster of canes that spread apart to form a ball-shaped bush.

CEPHALOTAXUS PLUM-YEW SUMMER

This grows very slowly inland where you just nip off straggly shoots when they mar the appearance of the shrub. In more favorable coastal locations, cut back the branches according to natural form. On narrow upright forms, cut back new growth halfway; thin weeping forms to feature picturesque branches. You can also shear this like a true yew.

CERCIDIPHYLLUM KATSURA-TREE LATE WINTER–SPRING

Thin out crowded branches and weak wood when leaves are off

PRUNING PLUS NATURE. As true cedars age, they lose their dense, cone shape and develop a high, flat crown. Here a few main limbs have been removed to expose the trunk and to emphasize the natural horizontal pattern of growth. As the top spreads even more, lower branches will be shaded out; then they must be removed. *Author photo* and you can see structure. This tree usually grows with several trunks and needs a little inside thinning but nothing more. In late spring, prune out the tiny dead twigs and the branches that have poor leaves, a condition common to trees growing on neutral or alkaline soil.

CERCIS REDBUD, JUDAS-TREE WINTER

Let alone, this develops a graceful, umbrella-shaped crown. But if you tamper with the branches, the tree is apt to become a dense unattractive globe—a real blot in the garden. Buy a multiple-trunked specimen if possible and let nature take its course. Short-lived and subject to decay, older trees require attention to keep them free of weak and dead wood. American redbud, *C. candensis,* offers a few problems. Asiatic redbud, *C. Siliquastrum,* suffers winter injury north of Zone 5. Chinese redbud, *C. chinensis,* becomes a thicket in unfavorable situations; thin this in winter, keeping just a few of the oldest, healthiest canes.

CESTRUM JESSAMINE CONTINUOUS

This produces suckers freely from the base; get rid of them with a sharp spade. If you grow shrubby species, cut branches going out of bloom to 6-inch stubs; it is the year-old shoots originating from near the base that bloom best. For better control of your plant—and for a better show of flowers—grow this as a wall shrub, fanned out flat or, better, twine it around a pillar. Pinch terminal shoots through the growing season to encourage branching; when a branch has shed its blooms, cut it back to a two- or three-leaf stub. This way, you can have flowers from top to bottom for a long time. You may wait to prune until after the display of berries but, in doing so, you will sacrifice some bloom.

CHAENOMELES JAPANESE QUINCE, FLOWERING QUINCE SUMMER–WINTER

Young bushes require little pruning; cut out weak canes to let in light and air. Rework old shrubs every four or five years. Remove several of the oldest canes, thin out weak and crowded shoots, and use a spade to cut out most of the suckers that surround the crown. Never shear or overprune because the shape is easily destroyed. The Chinese quince, *C. lagenaria* and its forms grow more or less upright, reaching to 10 feet. The Japanese quince, *C. japonica* and its forms are much lower and spread. Prune according to the natural habit of each. All, and particularly such hybrids as 'Knap Hill Scarlet' and 'Simonii', may be trained as wall shrubs. Fan out young branches flat against a trellis and remove any outward growth. Thin side branches so the wall is not entirely hidden. Trim summer shoots to four or five leaves, and shorten these to two buds the next winter. If fireblight attacks, immediately prune out any spring growth that withers, blackens, and looks scorched; cut deep into healthy wood. After each cut, dip clippers into a disinfectant solution.

CHAMAECYPARIS FALSE-CYPRESS SUMMER

Prune according to use and habit. Shear hedges two or three times through summer with sides sloped toward the top. Prune rock-garden miniatures frequently, pinching back leaders and thinning lateral branches to give plants a gnarled, alpine look. Leave unpruned, lawn specimens of *C. Lawsoniana,* the Sawara *C. pisifera,* and the Hinoki *C. obtusa;* or, to slow growth and thicken plants, clip off the new growth just at it matures. Clip bonsai specimens repeatedly through the growing season to shape them and maintain good color. Don't trim these potted miniatures when they are resting or dormant.

Chaste-tree see **VITEX**
Checker-berry see **GAULTHERIA**
Cherry see **PRUNUS**
Cherry-laurel see **PRUNUS Laurocerasus**
Chestnut see **CASTANEA**

CHIMONANTHUS praecox WINTERSWEET SUMMER

Every five or six years cut back the oldest canes to the ground. No other pinching or pruning is necessary except for the removal of diseased or dead wood, but who can resist cutting a few switches for the house in February? Brought into the house in midwinter, these bloom with a pervading sweetness that is the essence of spring. This shrub is reliably hardy through Zone 6, but you may grow it successfully farther north as a wall shrub. Get a rather large plant and set it in very good soil tight against a trellis on a sheltered south or east wall. Train it flat to the trellis, cut off any outward-growing branches, and reduce summer growth to three or four leaves.

Chinaberry-tree see **MELIA**
Chinese actinidia see **ACTINIDIA**
Chinese scholar-tree see **SOPHORA**

CHIONANTHUS FRINGE-TREE, OLD-MAN'S-BEARD

SUMMER–WINTER

Grow as a shrub or small tree with several trunks. The single-trunk method is dangerous because when borers attack, and these often do, the plant may be lost. Cut off spent flowers of the male tree but don't clean up female trees until birds have finished with the blue-black fruit in early winter. The American *C. virginica,* as well as the Chinese *C. retusa,* need little pruning but branches may be cut for the house. Try to maintain a natural rather than a shaped form. Take drastic measures for borers. Cut back badly infested trunks to the ground and burn them. Then apply a root-absorbing systemic insecticide to the soil. If you have a borer-infested single-stem specimen, use a wood-carving gouge to dig out the borer and the tunnelled wood; then seal the holes with tree-wound dressing. Soon basal shoots will appear; thin to keep only three of four. Cut out the old trunk entirely and grow your plant as a bush.

USEFUL FORM FOR A FRINGE-TREE. This specimen tree has been pruned to form an entryway feature. Some branches were chosen for special functions, the low ones toward the door to give privacy for a guest-room window, the long one on the far right to catch the illumination of a garden night-light. *Miner photo for Helen Van Pelt Wilson*

FRINGE-TREE IN BLOOM. The value of pruning with a purpose, as in the previous picture, is realized when the fringe-tree, flowering in its allotted space, blooms low to fill house and garden with fragrance. *Miner photo* for *Home Garden*

CHOISYA ternata MEXICAN-ORANGE SUMMER

Prune this tender, sweet-scented, broadleaf evergreen to a rather formal shape; clip back succulent shoots that reach beyond the body of the plant, and remove one or two of the oldest canes at the ground every second or third year. Grown as a tubbed specimen in the North, it tolerates shearing, but don't try to keep it below 4 to 5 feet.

Chokeberry see **ARONIA**

Christmas-berry see **PHOTINIA**
Cinquefoil see **POTENTILLA**

CISTUS ROCK-ROSE SUMMER

Open up the large growers—those that exceed 3 feet—by removing ingrowing twigs and inside weak branches. Clip back the low spreading kinds after they have flowered. A suitable site is essential. If your plants are lank with lots of dead wood, move them to a well-drained, stony rock ledge that is sun drenched; there they will fill out and become thrifty. No amount of pruning will make good specimens if plants are growing in an unfavorable place.

CITRUS ORANGE, GRAPEFRUIT, LEMON, LIME, CALAMONDIN SPRING–SUMMER

At planting time, thin out your young tree to three of four well-spaced branches and head-back these scaffold arms to equal lengths. Allow two or three more branches to form in the next two to three years; then remove the leader. This method of pruning produces a low, ball-shaped tree. Future pruning consists of removing in-growing, rubbing, and crowding branches as they develop. Older, rangy trees can be worked down gradually; drop-prune (Chapter 2) two or three of the largest, upright branches each summer, cutting out high limbs with wrist-sized butts. If too many sprouts appear below the cut, thin them while they are still tender and green. (You may want to experiment with cleft-grafting improved citrus cultivars into stubbed-back branches, particularly if your tree is of a not too good variety.) Bearing citrus trees of good scaffold form require little annual pruning, though excessively vigorous new shoots may be pinched back in early spring. If you are seriously interested in the fine points of citrus production read the bulletins of the U.S. Department of Agriculture and your own state university. Species and cultivars vary greatly in growth form; accordingly, refined techniques of training have been worked out for locally favored kinds.

Potted citrus plants tend to go dormant in winter but growth resumes in early spring. To control a plant's shape and size, pinch new shoots as they appear. You may shear standard forms. The calamondin has gained favor as a specimen for bonsai training. Meyer lemon, the Ponderosa lemon, and the Tahitian lime make good pot plants. Given regular feedings and proper exposure, these bloom and bear when kept to 3 feet or even less. Thin the branches and head-back overly strong shoots so your potted citrus resembles a mature tree rather than an ill-kept bush. Heavy pinching is necessary during periods of active growth.

CLEMATIS VIRGIN'S-BOWER, JAPANESE CLEMATIS

SPRING–SUMMER–WINTER

When you plant a vine, immediately cut it back to two or three pairs of buds (joints) unless you have a very weak plant, then cut back more, to a single pair. Because of wide differences in growth habit and season of bloom, time your pruning and adapt it to type. But to prune any kind, you must loosen the clinging leaf tendrils. After pruning, use strips of soft cloth to secure the vine to its support until new leaves are formed to hold it. Never kink a clematis or fasten it with wire. Through late spring and early summer, induce branching by pinching out tips of growing shoots. Also pinch out new crown shoots to stimulate leafing out at the base.

A large group that blooms on old wood includes *C. alpina, C. Armandii.* 'Barbara Jackman', 'Belle of Woking', *C. chrysocoma,* 'Daniel Deronda', 'Duchess of Edinburgh', 'Edouard Desfosse', *C. florida,* 'Lady Londesborough', 'Lasurstern', *C. macropetala,* 'Marcel Moser', *C. montana,* 'Mrs George Jackman', 'Nelly Moser', *C. patens, C. Spooneri,* and 'The President'. Train these strong growers to prevent tangling; thin out weak branches; pinch back vigorous shoots so as to develop neat, attractive vines. Where two strong growths break from the same joint or those adjoining, pinch out both to prevent one from driving the other into dormancy. In spring, when buds are well swollen, trim out all dead wood but leave it in place as support for new growth.

The Lanuginosa group, blooming early from last year's growth or later from new growth, includes: 'Beauty of Richmond', 'Beauty of Worcester', 'Elsa Spaeth', 'Fairy Queen', 'Henryi', 'Lady Northcliffe', 'Lord Nelville', 'Marie Boisselot', 'Mrs. Cholmondeley', 'Mrs. Hope', 'Prins Hendrik', 'W. E. Gladstone', and 'William Kennett'. For early flowering, prune sparingly as with the group above. If you want a great show of summer flowers, prune hard as for the groups below. Hard pruning results in bushier plants.

The Jackmanii and Viticella groups that bloom vigorously on new

PRUNING A CLEMATIS VINE. Figure 1 shows an established vine. To thicken it, cut back *both* branches at A and B; (if you cut back only one, it will go dormant and all energy will go to making shoots from the buds on the other branch). At C only one side shoot appears; leave it alone or cut back higher up as needed. It this were a new vine, it should be cut back at D at planting time, and cuts also made at A and B. Figure 2 shows typical mechanical injury to clematis; at A the branch has been kinked during manipulation and the bark twisted away from the wood. Cut such injured shoots back to uninjured wood just beyond a joint. At B the stem has been broken, by a sharp bend or nicked by a pruning tool. Cut back the stem to healthy buds just below at C.

Figure 1

Figure 2

wood include: 'Abundance', *C. alba, C. ascotiensis,* 'Comtesse de Bouchaud', 'Ernest Markham', 'Gipsy Queen', 'Huldine', *C. Jackmanii, C. kermesina.* 'Lady Betty Balfour', 'Little Nell', 'Madame Edouard André', 'Minuet', 'M. Koster', 'Perle d'Azur', 'Royal Velours', *C. venosa,* 'Victoria', 'Ville de Lyon', and *C. Viticella.* Each spring cut them back to within 6 inches of last year's wood. Some will send up new shoots from the crown. As these appear, cut back all old wood to the ground. If much old wood is kept, less and less new flowering wood will develop. The familiar, fragrant Japanese clematis, *C. paniculata,* blooms early in fall, on new growth that reaches to 10 feet or more in one season. Cut it back in winter to 2 to 3 feet.

The Texensis group includes, besides the species *C. texensis* 'Countess of Onslow', 'Grace Darling', 'Gravetye Beauty'. When buds swell in spring, cut back to live growth. Or, if vigorous shoots push out from the crown, cut old wood to the ground and, as they appear, pinch new shoots. Rampant species, as *C. Jouiniana* and *C. tangutica,* require little pruning. In mid-spring remove dead wood and thin out the tangle of vines every two or three years. Watch these for dominant shoots. Pinch these to preserve a full, balanced plant.

Treat the non-climbing *C. recta* and *C. manshurica* like herbaceous perennials. Cut them to the ground after frost. Pinch out half of the spring shoots to develop full, pillar plants with prolonged bloom.

CLETHRA SWEET-PEPPERBUSH, LILY-OF-THE-VALLEY-TREE SUMMER

For best flowers and fuller growth, cut spent blooming wood to the ground as soon as flowers fade; at the same time, cut out most of the new crop of suckers with a sharp spade, saving a few to develop into next year's flowering wood. Or you may prune lightly for an informal, open bush. After you prune, apply a deep, porous, acid mulch—decayed oak leaves or acid peatmoss—to protect the crown and produce good flowering wood for next year. The American *C. alnifolia* and some thirty other worthwhile species from China and Japan are all surface rooted, vigorous, and inclined to bloom from year-old wood. In moist, rich soil, they quickly form large clumps as they sucker freely at the base. Some Asiatic types reach tree size and can be pruned to grow as single-trunk specimens. The tender Madeira lily-of-the-valley-tree, *C. arborea,* is evergreen. In the Deep South, it may be grown as a tree or very large shrub.

Cobnut see **CORYLUS**

CODIAEUM variegatum CROTON SPRING–SUMMER
This may develop a dead stub when a branch is cut back, or a broomy cluster of new shoots may break out; either condition is unsightly. Therefore govern shape by pinching out the tips of new shoots to encourage branching and by rubbing off buds that begin to break where a branch is undesirable. If your old shrub is tall and leggy, reduce it by cutting a third or more of the canes to the ground with a lopper. Feed the plant to encourage new basal shoots and pinch these frequently to develop low branches. Then gradually remove the remainder of the older branches. Potted crotons are more or less dormant through winter. In early spring wake them up with a weekly feeding of liquid fertilizer and a daily syringing. As growth resumes, pinch the new tips to keep the plant compact. If your potted plant is leggy, you may air-layer it (see your garden encyclopedia for the method). In midsummer, you may root the cuttings taken from shoots that break from the old stump in a perlite-filled flat covered with clear plastic.

COLUTEA BLADDER-SENNA SPRING–WINTER
While shrubs are dormant, reduce last summer's growth to about half. Allow plenty of time to do this, and count on lots of hand labor, particularly with twiggy types, but this way you can build up a well-proportioned, moderately compact shrub that will bloom profusely. Think twice before you remove a main trunk to the ground; plants seldom require such severe pruning and, unless several, young, well-formed canes are present to maintain the plant, you will ruin your shrub. Many kinds are rather tender. Although they produce their yellow, orange, copper, or brick-colored flowers on new wood, a little pruning, as buds break in spring, may be in order to remove winter-damaged twigs. When pruning, stay with the natural form of the shrub; the familiar *C. arborescens* grows loose and open; *C. orientalis* and *C. istria* are twiggy and inclined to be too dense.

Coral-tree see **ERYTHRINA**
Coral-vine see **ANTIGONON**
Cork-tree see **PHELLODENDRON**

Cornelian-cherry see **CORNUS**

CORNUS DOGWOOD, CORNELIAN-CHERRY SPRING–SUMMER–WINTER

For pruning purposes, dogwood is considered in four categories: the large-flowered trees—*C. florida, C. Kousa,* and *C. Nuttallii;* thc small-flowered trees, *C. officinalis* and *C. mas* (though this often grows as a large bush); the large shrubby *C. alternifolia* and *C. Amomum* and their varieties; and the so-called osiers with their colorful winter bark. The large tree dogwoods need little pruning. Their beauty depends on natural, unaltered growth; at maturity limbs often sweep to the ground. The tree has a layered effect that injudicious pruning may ruin but careful thinning out will enhance the horizontal pattern. Remove weak, inner limbs as they become shaded out; very early in spring, prune away any dead or injured wood; when trees are in flower or right afterwards, remove crossing and interfering limbs. You can always wait for full flowering to remove branches that overhang walks or interfere with mowing. Then you can use the lovely cut branches for house decoration. Be sure to prune to a secondary branch or to the trunk, and paint all cuts.

Prune *C. mas* even less, also *C. officinalis,* its look-alike relative with no common name. In winter, remove dead wood and crowded branches. You may cut arm-loads of flowering branches in February or March without damaging these species, but use sharp clippers and leave no stubs. Prune the bushy rough-twig dogwoods, the gray-bark dogwoods, and other large shrub-forms used for informal screens and wild-life shelter like other flowering shrubs; remove five- or six-year-old wood; keep basal sprouts in bounds with a spade and thin them out every year or two. You can also head these back by removing the tallest branches at a crotch somewhere below the crown. Prune in early spring as a compromise between losing a few flowers then and losing the berries later if you prune after flowering. Save those berries for the birds!

If you cut the osiers, as *C. alba, C. stolonifera,* and *C. sanguinea,* and their forms to the ground every year and fertilize heavily late in winter or early spring, you will get a strongly vertical swatch of vigorous, almost unbranched shoots. With the onset of winter these color brilliantly—blood or coral-red, vivid chartreuse-green or bright golden yellow. In summer, thin out weaker shoots that develop in older clumps. The purpose of such severe pruning, which results in just another green summer bush with negligible flowers and fruits, is to produce many year-old whips. These are the ones with the bright bark—glowing spots of color in a snowy winter garden. You may not want to prune forms with variegated foliage quite so hard; in winter, remove just a portion of the oldest wood. Through summer, head-back the most vigorous shoots; at the same time, thin out most of the basal sprouts. This treatment produces a broad, nicely filled shrub.

Since tree forms of dogwood readily decay, prune with clean tools and seal cuts and abrasions at once with tree-wound dressing. Cut back osier and shrub forms with strong loppers; these need no wound treatment unless you cut out a very heavy trunk.

CORYLOPSIS WINTER-HAZEL SPRING

Once or twice a decade after flowering, cut a few of the oldest trunks to the ground; also cut out weak and crowded twigs at a crotch. North of Zone 6, you can grow this shrub against a wall; prune it as a rather narrow open column, or fan it out on a trellis, clipping off any out-reaching branches. *C. Wilsonii* will grow as a small, gnarled, ornamental tree but you will be kept busy cutting out basal shoots for some years until a mature trunk dominates the plant. The Japanese *C. spicata* is best for wall use.

CORYLUS HAZELNUT, FILBERT, COBNUT EARLY SPRING

Prune according to habit and use. Tree forms—*C. Colurna, C. chinensis, C. Fargesii,* and *C. Sieboldiana*—only require removal of weak or damaged wood and some thinning of crowded and interfering branches. These handsome species are easily ruined by a prune-happy gardener. Grown as ornamental shrubs, they need more attention. Prune purple-leaved nut, *C. maxima purpurea,* at the ground only. If you cut back a branch, you will get a veritable witch's broom. Take off old canes to the ground and cut back and thin out suckers with a spade.

To keep open crowns on ornamental forms of *C. Avellana,* cut out most of the suckers in spring. Every second or third year, remove old canes from established plants of the golden-leaf nut, *C. Avellana aurea,* and the cutleaf nut, *C. Avellana heterophylla.* Heavily prune out twigs from the grotesquely twisted and gnarled *C. Avellana contorta* to feature trunks and branches. Space side branches widely and cut out any that are not notably crooked. To emphasize character, you may wish to reduce this species to a single trunk or, at most, three trunks. Through summer, sprouts break vigorously from the understock on which the species is often grafted. Push back the soil with a trowel and use a sharp knife to cut out the sprouts where they originate.

Don't try to prune native hazelnuts and filberts for low branching; their growth habit is vase-shaped, with the crown carried high above a sheaf of almost unbranched trunks, and no amount of whacking back will change this. Every four or five years, cut out most of the oldest canes from a clump and remove enough of the younger ones to keep the basal crown somewhat open. Treat European nuts, grown in bush-form, the same way.

For commercial nut production, European filberts and cobnuts are grown in tree-form. As soon as you set them out, prune young plants to three or four well-spaced side branches with wide crotches. Then shorten the branches to equal length. You will be busy cutting out basal shoots for several years, but it is important not to let any sprouts remain through a growing season. As a young tree develops, allow it to have six or seven widely branched laterals; then remove the leader. Until nut production begins, take out only in-growing shoots. The crop is produced on wood of the previous year. In early spring, remove a fair amount of old terminal growth to encourage development of new shoots for production a year later. You will then be cutting off this year's bearing wood, so pruning is a compromise based on the strength of the tree, on this year's crop, and next year's crop. To control basal suckers on bearing trees, pull back the soil during the summer so you can cut out sprouts while they are still soft and green; replace the soil in fall. With age, the number of suckers is reduced.

COTINUS SMOKE-TREE SUMMER

Cut back young trees severely to force the development of three or four main trunks. When your tree is moved in, trim and paint injured roots before it is set, and afterwards clip off all new growth for at least one season. These weak-rooted shrubs are difficult to transplant but require little attention once they are established. The American type, *C. americanus,* is columnar; if a branch is sprung outward by snow or other agency, try tying it back in place with strips of soft cloth; if the branch does not stay after six weeks or so, cut it out at a crotch. The European *C. Coggygria* is shorter and more spreading; it needs no pruning other than removal of dead wood. Prune the elegant purple-leaved forms rather severely after they are moved. Watch for green-leaved suckers breaking out of the understock and remove these while they are still tender. A clean cut with a sharp knife is the way to do it.

COTONEASTER SPRING–SUMMER–WINTER

These shrubs vary from limp, prostrate miniatures through many sizes and shapes to small tree-forms. We can generalize on pruning because little is required. Prune deciduous kinds in winter, taking out twiggy, crowded growth. Removing the oldest trunks at the crown usually takes care of this. Cut back old, disproportionate branches to a crotch, bringing the shrub into balance; shorten young, unbranched whips to just a few buds. Some of the newer hybrid forms, when growing vigorously, send up succulent summer canes; while these are short, pinch them once or twice to slow down growth and encourage branching.

Prune evergreen kinds in mid-spring just as old leaves fall and before new foliage expands. If a plant seems crowded, take out a few of the oldest branches and cut back last year's growth to make it conform to a good shape. Some of the evergreens, particularly in the rockspray group, produce long unbranched whips. In a season or two, these fill out with well-formed lateral branches to make a larger shrub, but you may pinch them back as they develop if you want to keep your bush small.

Cut back halfway a newly set hedge of *C. Simonsii, C. divaricata,* or *C. apiculata.* Shear as it looks ragged, giving the sides a pronounced inward slope toward the top; then sun can reach the lowest branches. Some, especially rocksprays, can be trained as wall shrubs. Fan out the main trunks and remove all out-growing branches and also those growing in toward the wall. Also remove enough side branches to allow the wall to show through the plant. Pinch back summer shoots to five or six leaves and shorten these during the winter to two buds. If fireblight blackens new growth, remove the shoot, cutting *at least* a foot below any sign of the disease. Select a promising lateral to replace the severed branch. Before making a second cut, dip the clippers in a strong household disinfectant.

Cottonwood see **POPULUS**

Crabapple see **MALUS**
Cranberry see **VACCINIUM**
Cranberry-bush see **VIBURNUM**
Crape-myrtle see **LAGERSTROEMIA**

CRATAEGUS HAWTHORN SUMMER–WINTER

Shear hedges through summer but leave ornamental specimens alone. Nibbling away at a tree without understanding its growth habit is a sure way to ruin it. Young trees may be almost columnar; with age they spread wide, and a fine old mature specimen may be twice as broad as it is tall, drooping right to the ground. The *only* way to take wood from a hawthorn is by drop-pruning (Chapter 2). Follow the branch you wish to remove down to a crotch and cut it away. If that does not improve the shape, follow down again to the next crotch and make another cut. A stubbed-off branch grows a crop of switches that can never be made to look right. Don't worry about V-shaped crotches; the wood is strong and trees seldom split apart.

Cross-vine see **BIGNONIA**
Croton see **CODIAEUM variegatum**
Crowberry see **EMPETRUM**

CRYPTOMERIA JAPANESE-CEDAR SUMMER

Prune large specimens only to correct broken or winter-damaged branches; if you shear them severely (an unfortunate custom on the West Coast), you lose the elegance of the foliage. You may *lightly* shear young specimens for a few years to tighten them, or, for a less artificial look, clip back each branch; this will retain the graceful undulation of the plant. Bonsai growers favor *C. japonica Lobbii*, *C. japonica sinensis*, and *C. japonica pungens*. Don't disturb these when they are dormant but with tweezers pick out most of the new growth in spring, a bit at a time, before it hardens off.

Cucumber-tree see **MAGNOLIA**

CUPRESSUS CYPRESS SUMMER

Special forms, such as the Chinese weeping cypress, *C. funebris,* and the Kashmir cypress, *C. cashmeriana* (often erroneously called *C. pendula*), need the touch of an expert in thinning branches to develop a very open "Chinese silk painting" tree. Shear the common Italian type when young to make it dense; leave adult trees alone. These tender evergreens, strongly columnar in form, may be pot grown in the North; every year with a sharp spade cut out the edge of the root ball a third way round. Make the cut about 2 inches in from the container, pry out the tangle of roots and soil, and replace with sandy, gritty loam. Work round the pot in the course of three years.

Currant see **RIBES**
Cypress see **CUPRESSUS**

CYTISUS BROOM SPRING

Cut back spring-blooming sorts immediately after flowering. Cut out half to two-thirds of the wood that bore flowers, using hand-clippers rather than shears. (Shearing a broom ruins its form.) In the same way, early in spring, prune late-summer and fall-bloomers. To make them bushy, hand-clip young plants two or three times through the first two summers. When plants get leggy and develop quantities of dead wood, interplant with young ones for you cannot rejuvenate old plants.

DABOECIA IRISH HEATH SUMMER–FALL

In June after this blooms, cut back flower-bearing stems, and again in September as summer flowers dwindle. St. Daboec's heath, *D. cantabrica* and its cultivars may reach 2 feet; thin out the wood on dense plants to reveal a little of trunk and branches. *D. azorica* and forms are low and creeping; remove any stems that overlay the crown before the covered portion is smothered. If your plants are sparse, constantly dying back here and there, check the soil; it should be well drained, a quite acid peat-sand mixture. Pruning will not produce a well-furnished plant grown in the wrong type of soil.

DAHLIA

Too much emphasis has been placed on producing blooms for competition and not enough on plants as garden ornamentals. They are heavy feeders and also require plenty of water; given these, and enough space, they can be grown as large clumps or as single, branched canes. European gardeners often set undivided clumps in beds, staking a cluster of half a dozen stalks, each of which has been pinched to achieve a great "bush" of blooms. Another way is to

DIRECTING DAHLIA GROWTH. When a stalk has two or three pairs of mature (compound) leaves, pinch out the tip, as shown. Then side shoots will break vigorously and produce several canes to make a bushy plant. If these show too early flower buds, as on this plant, remove the buds and the shoot will continue to develop.

plant single tubers, allow one stalk to develop on each and pinch that when it has developed a few leaves—two sets for the large A types, three sets for B and smaller sorts. Laterals will break below the pinched tip, four where two sets of leaves remain, six where three sets of leaves are left on the original stalk. Keep in mind that the more bulk you allow a plant to develop, the more fertilizer and water you must give it. And staking is important; set a heavy stake when you plant the tuber and use strips of soft rag to keep every stem firmly supported. You *can* pinch dahlias to control flower production for show purposes. It takes twenty-five to thirty days for a bud to develop into a bloom. If your plant shows large buds a month before a show, pinch them out and let only one lateral develop from the first pair of leaves. Refinements of this technique are discussed in specialized texts on dahlia culture.

DAPHNE SPURGE-LAUREL, MEZEREON SPRING

Prune far down the spent flower shoots of the evergreen garland daphne, *D. Cneorum;* then plants will produce new growth for another crop or two of bloom. Also shear back after bloom the evergreen hybrid, *D. Burkwoodii* and the winter daphne, *D. odora.* Leave the deciduous February daphne, *D. Mezereum* and *D. Gwenka,* strictly alone. The trick with daphne is culture, not pruning; grow in sun, provide good drainage, gritty soil with some peat, and *plenty of lime.* Then you will have no dead wood to cut out.

Date-plum see **DIOSPYROS**

DAVIDIA DOVE-TREE WINTER

Prune as little as possible. Maintain a leader on young plants by shortening side branches halfway on the current year's growth. Or grow multiple-stemmed. Then thin out side branches, removing most of the inside ones while they are small to expose the trunk pattern here and there. Use clippers with discretion for this tree does not heal well nor is it a strong grower.

DEUTZIA SPRING–SUMMER

Subject to winter injury, this shrub requires a good going over as buds swell in spring to get rid of dead twigs. After flowers fade, cut out a few of the oldest canes at the ground and cut some other old canes back to promising tufts of leaves low in the plant. As new shoots are produced at the basal crown and low on old wood through summer, pinch out tips to encourage branching. Low arching species, as *D. gracilis* and *D. kalmiaeflora* only require removal of some of the oldest wood every five years or so. The upright *D. Lemoinei* and *D. scabra* need an annual going over to keep them well furnished with foliage close to the base.

Devil's-walking-stick see **ARALIA**
Dewberry see **RUBUS**

DIERVILLA BUSH-HONEYSUCKLE (not weigela) LATE SPRING–SUMMER

As flowers fade, remove hard, twiggy old wood; cut back to the basal crown or to a joint where buds are breaking. Pinch new shoots repeatedly through summer to encourage low branching. *D. Lonicera* spreads out naturally from the crown to about 4 feet, *D. sessilifolia* attains 5 feet, and *D. rivularis* may reach 6 feet. Don't try to grow these below their normal height. To cover a steep sunny bank peg down branches of *D. sessilifolia;* it produces stolons that quickly thicken up a planting. But you can surely find something better for garden display than these rather harsh native bushes.

DIOSPYROS PERSIMMON, KAKI, DATE-PLUM WINTER

Encourage the terminal shoot of a young tree by nipping back side shoots halfway to the top. With this treatment, a huge columnar tree will develop in time. Or, to get a zigzag, gnarled, Oriental effect, grow the American species, *D. virginiana,* to about 10 feet; then remove the leader and trim back side branches to selected branchlets. The Oriental, *I. Kaki,* may be grown unpruned as a rather large shade tree or trimmed like a peach (see *Prunus*) to keep fruit close to the ground. The quite tender date-plum, *D. Lotus,* is usually grown as a small, gnarled, unpruned tree.

Dogwood see **CORNUS**
Douglas-fir see **PSEUDOTSUGA Douglasii**
Dove-tree see **DAVIDIA**

DURANTA PIGEON-BERRY, GOLDEN DEWDROP CONTINUOUS

Grow this frost-sensitive plant as a shrub or small tree; lavender flowers, followed by showy yellow fruit, are borne on year-old wood. To keep new wood coming, cut back a few of the oldest branches on shrub-forms to 3- or 4-inch stubs several times through the year; when new shoots arise from the stubs, pull off all but one or two. If your specimen is tree-form, drop-prune (Chapter 2) the longest branches to encourage renewal from low in the scaffold; do not stub-back a branch or an unlovely brush of shoots will break just behind the cut. If your plant gets frosted, watch for loose bark and cut back beyond it to healthy growth.

Dutchman's pipe see **ARISTOLOCHIA**
Dwarf pomegranate see **PUNICA Granatum nana**

ELAEAGNUS OLEASTER, RUSSIAN-OLIVE, SILVER-BERRY SUMMER

Prune tree-forms to expose the dramatic twisted trunks; thin branches to lighten the leaf load; remove water sprouts for limbs and trunk. If basal sprouts come up, carefully trowel away the soil from the trunk to expose points of origin; then slice them off clean with a sharp knife and paint the cuts. Since more suckers will arise from damaged tissue, keep your cutting to a minimum. When root sprouts appear in the lawn, cut them out with a sharp spade or try to pull them out after heavy rain. If your Russian-olive, *E. angustifolia,* develops a virulent disease in early summer with whole branches drooping, leaves turning brown, and twigs shriveling, use your pruning saw to cut out all diseased portions. I have seen trees cut back to stumps that regained health and looks over a five-year period. But you must act promptly before the entire tree is lost, and be sure to dip your pruners in a disinfectant solution between cuts.

Prune bush-forms—*E. multiflora, E. pungens* and *E. umbellata*—just after they bloom. Every four or five years as they show signs of deterioration, cut out the oldest wood. In summer, nip back new growth halfway. Avoid heavy pruning which results in a terrific crop of basal suckers that are hard to control. If forms of *E. pungens* with variegated foliage throw an all-green branch, remove it immediately.

Elderberry see **SAMBUCUS**
Elm see **ULMUS**

ELSHOLTZIA SUMMER

Cut back leafy shoots that have flowered to one-third their length. Prune *E. Stauntonii,* the only commonly grown member of this genus, lightly or it will go into decline. Replace deteriorating specimens rather than trying to rework them.

EMPETRUM CROWBERRY AUTUMN

Clip back newly set plants of this rock-loving creeper. If it likes your garden, it will develop into a dense carpet of plants 12 inches high with a spread of 2 feet. Cut back straggly ends in fall but no real pruning is required.

Empress-tree see **PAULOWNIA**
English ivy see **HEDERA Helix**

ENKIANTHUS EARLY SPRING–SUMMER

In spring, lop off half the old wood of failing plants to force new basal shoots. With bushy specimens, pinch low shoots through summer to encourage branching. Also pinch new growth at the top for control instead of clipping. Take advantage of the leggy, open-topped tendency of these beauties by planting them for height in the azalea bed. Trim them as open shrubs with bare trunks and exposed branches; you will be delighted with the fall foliage color against the dark trunks.

ERICA HEATH (not heather) SPRING

These acid-loving evergreen shrubs vary from almost prostrate forms to the so-called tree-heath that grows from 12 to 20 feet in its Mediterranean habitat. Just clip spent blooms from tree-heath and tender species, as *E. Cavendishiana, E. grandiflora,* and *E. hyemalis.* Prune garden plants like *E. carnea* after flowering, cutting back spent bloom spikes. At the same time, remove older upright stalks topped with brooms of twiggy growth to prevent their lying over the heart of the plant and smothering it. Severely reduce rampant plants that tend to crowd nearby varieties of more restricted growth. If a green shoot appears in a gold- or bronze-leaved form, clip it out before it dominates the weaker color variant.

ERIOBOTRYA japonica LOQUAT CONTINUOUS

This very tender plant with fragrant white panicles of autumn flowers, followed by fruit in spring, grows in the open garden in the South or as a tubbed plant in the North. In the South, named cultivars are planted for high-quality fruit. To thicken growth, pinch unbranched garden trees when they are about waist-high, and pinch new shoots at 15 inches, unless you see developing buds in leaf axils—these will become branches later—or if flower buds are evident. Remove crossing branches inside the tree, and cut back to a crotch any that disturb the symmetry of the crown.

Potted loquats look best as rather formal, well-thinned specimens that feature the graceful branches and large, bold-textured leaves; but they may be grown bush-form. Then you need only cut out inside branches that are weak or crowded. Pinch the new shoots at the three- or four-leaf stage. If it is necessary to remove a branch for appearance, make a sharp, close cut; then use a small woodworking gouge to reduce the stub to a slight indentation. This will bark over smoothly with no discernible scar. Culture is the trick with potted specimens. They require a rich, coarse, potting medium; weekly applications of dilute fertilizer in periods of active growth; bright sun; and daily syringing of foliage.

ERYTHRINA CORAL-TREE, FLAME-TREE WINTER

These tender, thorny, woody plants vary from 3 feet (*E. herbacea*) to 60 feet, (*E. indica*). Common in Florida and southern California are *E. Crista-gallii* and *E. Corallodendrum* grown as gnarled, drooping,

TUB-GROWN LOQUAT. This specimen has been well pruned to a clean uncluttered trunk and uncrossed inner branches with a crown of leaves that are nicely spaced. Now the small evergreen tree is at just the right stage for pinching out some terminal leaf clusters. At this stage, there will be no scarring and this pinching checks growth for a time and encourages branching. *Guy Burgess photo*

or spreading specimens. Cut lower limbs back to a crotch for clearance from below and thin out the main limbs to feature the bleached, "driftwood" appearance of the bark. No regular pruning is needed, but drop-prune (Chapter 2) as necessary to remove rubbing or crowded branches.

ESCALLONIA WINTER–SUMMER

These tender Chilean shrubs are mostly evergreen, enduring no frost, though deciduous *E. Philippiana* is hardy to Washington, D. C. Pinch basal shoots to encourage low branching, then, on older shrubs, to encourage basal renewal, cut back about half the wood each winter to a very low crotch. *Never* stub-back a branch. In frost-free climates, you may grow *E. macrantha* as a 6-foot, sheared, evergreen hedge. Soon after flowers fade, take off the persistent seed pods that mar the looks of the plant.

EUONYMUS BURNING-BUSH, SPINDLE-TREE, STRAWBERRY-BUSH WAHOO SPRING–MIDSUMMER

Grow the deciduous *E. europaeus, E. americanus, E. latifolius, E. sachalinensis, E. alatus, E. atropurpureus,* their forms, and the less common species in semishade as rather large open bushes or as small trees. Take out an occasional awkward branch or borer-infested cane. With a sharp spade, cut out any suckers from the roots. If there is considerable dieback, chances are it is due to scale; try a systemic insecticide to clean this up.

Prune according to use the evergreen *E. Fortunei, E. japonicus,* and *E. patens* that vary from trailing to above 7-foot plants with foliage from thumbnail size to 3 inches or more. These make excellent hedges and ground-covers but as specimen plants, sheared into globes and spotted around the lawn or among foundation Pfitzer junipers, they are unsightly and require clipping every two to three weeks to keep them trim.

Shear hedge and ground-cover plantings whenever they look ragged, but avoid late-summer pruning lest a rainy spell, followed by Indian summer, brings out new growth for frost to kill. If your hedge is out of shape, realign it by cutting off bulging old wood in early spring as the old leaves fall and before buds break. If your hedge appears worn out, try feeding and watering well for a full season; then early in spring, cut it back to 6-inch stubs. Sometimes good new growth is produced, sometimes plants fail to respond and die out; but it's worth the risk. Through the growing season shear off ground-covers. This is important because these upright shoots soon develop an adult habit, grow tall, becoming twiggy with smaller leaves, and tend to set flowers and fruit. Horizontal shoots will continue to creep or vine.

EUPHORBIA pulcherrima POINSETTIA SPRING

In frost-free gardens this familiar Christmas flower makes a striking appearance in the shrub border. Pruning is important if blooms are to be at their best. About May first, cut year-old stalks back to three buds. There will be one bud where a new stalk emerges from older wood, so you can easily see where to cut above the obvious second bud. You will then get fine long branches bearing large flowers. Old plants that have grown tall and woody can be brought back into shape by cutting them off about a foot above the ground with lopper or saw. As new shoots break, start cutting these back to the third bud, as above. On high, bare walls, an old trunk with heavy branches can be managed another way: stub-back the branches to make a vinelike pattern and thin out the shoots that develop. Because of the necessary quantity of old wood, flowers on such a plant won't be very large but the whole picture will be striking.

EXOCHORDA PEARL-BUSH EARLY SUMMER

These slow growers require little maintenance pruning. For good looks, remove faded flower spikes from specimen plants. In the shrub border, rejuvenate bushes every three or four years by removing about a third of the oldest wood, cutting cleanly to the ground. Basal shoots usually branch readily but through the growing season you may want to pinch young sprouts on vigorous, established plants to encourage low branching. Few basal suckers appear; cut these out with a sharp spade when you remove old wood.

FAGUS BEECH LATE WINTER–EARLY SPRING

The eight species include more than fifty forms—columnar, pyramidal, and weeping. Keep the upright, high-crowned type-species to a single leader. Remove interfering and rubbing branches that tend to develop throughout the life of all these trees. It is also essential to get rid of weak crotches by cutting back half on one side, as necessary; the wood is notoriously brittle and wide V-crotches split sooner or later. You cannot avoid the narrow crotches that develop in fastigiate forms (like poplars, narrowing toward the top) but the configuration of branches usually keeps them from splitting. Always remove sprung branches at a crotch. With weeping forms, thin out branches to reveal the writhing, silvery trunk and limbs. With hedges, cut back hard when you plant, shear in late winter or early spring, and again as new growth hardens off. Properly clipped, hedges grow 10 to 12 feet high, but can be restricted to a 15- to 18-inch width.

False-acacia see **ROBINIA**
False-buckthorn see **BUMELIA**
False-cypress see **CHAMAECYPARIS**
False-indigo see **AMORPHA**
False-spirea see **SORBARIA**

FICUS carica FIG SPRING–FALL

Figs are borne on new shoots and on year-old wood, the first crop on the older wood with more coming later on new wood. Prune toward a balanced amount of each. Where winters are mild, prune your young tree to four well-spaced side branches and remove the leader. Thereafter, trim out vigorous shoots that tend to fill the center of the tree and head-back strong new growths of the previous year. If new branches are produced too close together, remove some, although figs seldom require such thinning.

In marginal areas, try fanning out a tree on a sturdy trellis fastened a few inches from a south wall. Each spring reduce the previous year's growth to half, and remove any shoots growing straight out or back toward the wall. Thin side branches that want to overlap. Farther north, place your tree on a south wall and, when frost defoliates it, cut out most of the side branches, head-back the main canes (the plant will probably grow as a large bush), pull the branches into a tight bundle with soft cord, pack them with excelsior or other insulation, then wrap in burlap, and finally cover with plastic, perforated in a few places to let the bundle "breathe." In mid-spring undo the package and fan out the canes. Later, prune out those that refuse to break.

Cut back a newly set, potted fig to about 6 inches to force very low branches. Thin these to three or four, and cut them back to three leaves at the end of the first year. Overwinter in a frost-free cellar.

In spring, prune back last year's wood halfway; every second year, repot the plant in good topsoil, well reinforced with rotted manure or compost and bonemeal. Prune back main roots a foot or more when you repot. Through the growing season, feed monthly with a balanced pot-plant mixture.

Fig see **FICUS carica**
Filbert see **CORYLUS**
Fir see **ABIES**
Firethorn see **PYRACANTHA**
Five-leaf akebia see **AKEBIA**
Five-leaf aralia see **ACANTHOPANAX**
Flame-tree see **ERYTHRINA**
Flowering apricot see **PRUNUS**
Flowering cherry see **PRUNUS**
Flowering-maple see **ABUTILON**
Flowering plum see **PRUNUS**
Flowering quince see **CHAENOMELES**

FORSYTHIA GOLDEN-BELLS SPRING–SUMMER

This is a fine shrub on which to practice for it endures abuse and

GOING. This huge old 'Spring Glory' forsythia has got away from the gardener, though it makes a fine screen for the front porch. *Philpott photo*

GONE. Leggy and unlovely, the newly pruned forsythia offers little beauty (and such severe pruning is not recommended for many shrubs), but some heavy green buds are already breaking out at the base. *Philpott photo*

COMING BACK. New shoots are pushing out at the base of the old forsythia and tips will be pinched out to encourage the low branching that makes a full bush. Notice buds breaking along the bare canes; they will clothe the stalks with foliage before summer arrives. *Philpott photo*

restores itself in two or three growing seasons. As flowers fade, cut off at the ground a few of the oldest canes; also clip back halfway drooping tips of mature wood to clear the lawn mower and prevent rooting. To encourage low branching through the summer, pinch back bright green, vigorous, new shoots that appear low in the plant. If these are not frequently stopped they develop into long, unbranched "fishing poles" by fall, ruining the appearance of the shrub.

Flowering types do not sucker. If you have the somewhat dwarf upright *F. viridissima bronxensis* (which blooms) or the drooping 'Arnold's Dwarf' (which doesn't, but roots easily from decumbent shoots), go through the plantings every spring to prune out any coarse, upright canes that mar the undulations of the mass. If you train erect species, as *F. Giraldiana* and others of similar habit, as wall plants to provide a golden window frame in February or March, take these down from the trellis after they flower, remove the twiggy wood and the oldest canes and then tie them up again. Don't pinch new shoots but train them to the trellis through summer.

When old neglected plants bloom sparsely and have become a thickened mass of heavy canes difficult to thin, cut the whole plant down to about a foot. Then remove the heaviest canes at the groundline, selecting three to five for survival. This is drastic but plants will make up to 2 feet of new growth by fall and there will be some bloom next spring. The second spring your forsythia will be handsome again.

FOTHERGILLA MID-SPRING

These native American shrubs bloom before leaves open. They require little pruning and no heading back. To prevent crowded growth, remove a few of the oldest canes at the ground every three or four years.

FRANKLINIA LATE AUTUMN

Contrary to much advice on cutting back, thinning, and pinching, this requires almost no pruning. If an occasional vigorous shoot breaks through the crown and sticks up, cut it back below the top growth. In time these awkward shoots branch and contribute to an elegant, free-form shrub that is as maintenance-free as any plant grown. Layer a few low branches to share plants with your friends.

FRAXINUS ASH EARLY WINTER

Prune a young tree rather severely to develop a clean, definite leader and a scaffold of well-spaced side branches with very wide crotches. Because this tree is brittle and liable to damage by wind or the weight of ice and wet snow, it is important to prune for sturdy branching. Strengthen the crotches of older trees by drop-pruning (Chapter 2) to remove excessive terminal growth. Also remove any vigorous shoots that break out below the crown and grow up through the top of the tree without branching. Columnar and fastigiate (narrowed) forms only require removal of branches that have sprung and are leaning out; cut these back to a crotch. Thin the weeping forms enough to feature the graceful contour of branches.

French-mulberry see **CALLICARPA**
Fringe-tree see **CHIONANTHUS**
Garden plum see **PRUNUS**

GAULTHERIA CHECKER-BERRY, LEMON-LEAF, SALAL, WINTERGREEN — LATE SPRING

These acid-loving, moisture demanding, broad-leaved evergreens resent almost any pruning. The dwarf shrubby kinds, grown in shady rock gardens and under ericaceous plantings, may be shaped by gentle late-spring pruning, and at Christmas you can cut sprays from the tiny, red-berried *G. procumbens* or wintergreen (if it grows in your garden), but otherwise it, too, is best left unpruned. To keep clumps of *G. Shallon,* the Northwest salal or lemon-leaf, in bounds, cut it back with a sharp spade and in late spring, remove a few of the oldest canes at the ground-line to stimulate new growth.

GENISTA BROOM — EARLY SUMMER

Brooms range from prostrate rock-garden forms to 20-foot species. All resent pruning and trimming is restricted to shearing young plants in nursery beds to make them branch well before mature wood forms. As flowers fade, it is possible to cut back the newest wood on old plants but little is gained by it. Although directions are often given for renovating old plants by cutting them back to the crown, I know of no authenticated instance of successful renewal of old plants. It is better to replace short-lived kinds as soon as they show deterioration.

Giant-reed see **ARUNDO donax**

GINKGO MAIDENHAIR-TREE MIDSUMMER

An immature tree is hardly attractive but don't try to improve it by pruning. Only time will make it ornamental. Cuts heal slowly; if you wound this tree, decay may set in. Better let it alone, whether you have the type-species, or a weeping, fastigiate, columnar, or pyramidal form.

GLEDITSIA HONEY-LOCUST WINTER

Young trees require considerable pruning, particularly some of the new, thornless, sterile cultivars that have a tendency to form weak crotches, and this tendency lasts for twenty years or longer. Wherever two equal-sized branches form a crotch, cut one back most of its length to a promising side branch or bud. Then the other will dominate and overcome any structural weakness. If awkward, upright shoots develop low in the branches of established trees, destroying symmetry and interfering with the crown system, cut them out where they originate and dress wounds carefully. Very old trees tend to go "staggy" in the top, the large, usually central branches dying back. As a safety measure, remove such trees even though in nature they may survive for decades. Almost all very old trees are hollow and filling cavities may only hasten decay. To try to save a tree, it may be better to clean out the rotted wood and spray or dust the cavity with an all-purpose garden mixture several times through the growing season.

Golden-bells see **FORSYTHIA**
Goldenchain-tree see **LABURNUM**
Golden dewdrop see **DURANTA**
Goldenrain-tree see **KOELREUTERIA**
Grape see **VITIS**
Grapefruit see **CITRUS**

GREVILLEA robusta SILK-OAK CONTINUOUS

This tender, lacy tree was once a popular conservatory specimen; now its brilliant flowers grace frost-free gardens. Drop-prune (Chapter 2) shrubby specimens to control height, but hold pruning to a minimum; it does little for form or vigor. When lowering a too tall specimen, cut the highest branches at crotches well down in the plant, but stagger heights to let the plant retain a fairly uniform density. Tree-forms tend to be pyramidal when young, but with no help at all take on curious, craggy, irregular shapes with age. Your only job is to remove lower branches for headroom and to repair broken limbs (the wood is brittle) by cutting them back to trunk or crotch.

Guelder-rose see **VIBURNUM**

GYMNOCLADUS dioica KENTUCKY COFFEE-TREE WINTER

On young trees, prune back side branches that interfere with the leader. Develop the beautiful winter silhouette of mature trees by thinning crowded branches; drop-prune (Chapter 2) to avoid stubs. By all means plant a male tree to avoid having a lawn full of big pods in fall; if root sprouts appear far and wide in the garden, reconcile yourself to getting a different species because for control, you would have to poison both sprouts and parent.

Hackberry see **CELTIS**

HALESIA SILVERBELL-TREE LATE SPRING

These ornamental native trees grown to one trunk need only a little pruning to keep them open and lacy, but you may wish to clip back new growth to slow increase in size or thin terminal wood to feature individual branches. Allow plenty of room for multiple-stemmed trees so that you will not have to try to reduce size unnaturally by heavy pruning; *H. carolina* grows to 25 feet; *H. monticola* to 75 feet.

HAMAMELIS WITCH-HAZEL SUMMER

Limit maintenance pruning to cutting winter branches for use in the house. To renovate a crowded bush, thin out and space the oldest canes, cutting some to the ground with loppers. If you want a small tree, select and stake one strong cane; remove all side branches for three or four years, and cut out basal sprouts. Then let a substantial branching top develop.

Hardhack see **SPIREA**
Hardy-orange see **PONCIRUS trifoliata**
Hawthorn see **CRATAEGUS**
Hazelnut see **CORYLUS**

Heath see **ERICA**
Heather see **CALLUNA**
Heavenly-bamboo see **NANDINA**

HEBE VERONICA EARLY SPRING–SUMMER

In the spring, remove straggly shoots of the previous year. Every fifteen years or so, prune heavily, cutting out at least half the oldest wood at the ground-line. If you grow these tender evergreen shrubs for a hedge, shear as needed, but not later than midsummer. Always slope sides sharply in toward the top so full sun reaches the bottom on both sides.

HEDERA Helix ENGLISH IVY SPRING–SUMMER

"Cut off tags," an old English text on gardening advises and that means clipping off the loose ends of vines. From the house wall cut off dangling pieces; in ground-covers cut off pieces that stick up or lay over, smothering the growth they cover. At least once each year, cut back wall ivy from windows and cornices. Then severely reduce new growth, cutting out any pieces that have pulled loose from a building. Old vines develop mature wood that is branchy and non-vining; it bears smooth oval leaves, flowering shoots, and berries. When pieces of this mature wood are rooted, the small plants—now called *Hedera Helix arborescens*—stay bushy and are fine for formal edgings. Clip them close and, if a vining shoot develops, cut it back hard.

Hedge-thorn see **CARISSA**
Hemlock see **TSUGA**
Hemp-tree see **VITEX**
Hercules-club see **ARALIA** or **ZANTHOXYLUM**

HIBISCUS MALLOW, ROSE-OF-SHARON, ALTHEA SPRING–WINTER–FALL

Prune woody, deciduous types, as rose-of-Sharon, *H. syriacus,* in winter; thin crowded branches inside the bush by cutting to a crotch. For standards (tree-forms), lay back the soil and cut off tender basal suckers with a sharp knife. Use a spade to thin out suckers around bushes. In late summer, allow half a day to pick off all seed pods; otherwise young plants will sprout all over the garden.

Late in fall, cut back the herbaceous rose-mallow and its hybrids.

Lay the cut stalks over the crown and mound with compost. Uncover in spring; when new shoots are kneehigh, pull out crowded and weak ones. In early spring, heavily prune tender varieties grown in tubs in the North, outdoors in the South. Reduce all new side growth by two-thirds and cut out strong vertical shoots. When young plants are established, cut them back to 6 inches; pinch side shoots frequently through the first growing season.

Hickory see **CARYA**
Holly see **ILEX**
Holly-olive see **OSMANTHUS**

HOLODISCUS ROCK-SPIREA SUMMER

To prevent seeding, trim these lightly as flower-heads fade. With loppers, thin out the crown at the ground-line; if suckers come up around the plant, dig them out with a sharp spade.

Honey-locust see **GLEDITSIA**
Honeysuckle see **LONICERA**
Hop-hornbeam see **OSTRYA**
Hop-tree see **PTELEA trifoliata**
Hop-vine see **AMPELOPSIS**
Hornbeam see **CARPINUS**
Horse-chestnut see **AESCULUS**
Hortensia see **HYDRANGEA**
Huckleberry see **VACCINIUM**

HYDRANGEA SNOWBALL, HORTENSIA, PEEGEE EARLY SPRING–LATE FALL

Since the species vary greatly in form and hardiness, only common kinds are discussed here. Late each fall, cut hills-of-snow, *H. arborescens grandiflora,* to the ground; pile the cut stems over the crown and mound with old, rotted manure or coarse compost for winter protection. In spring, remove the stems, but leave the manure. As new shoots emerge, pull out weak and crowded ones. You can grow the peegee, *H. paniculata grandiflora,* and the earlier *H. paniculata praecox,* in bush-form, but they look better as very small trees, formal standards, or in loose clumps of strong old stems with irregular heads of flowering wood. In early spring, cut back year-old shoots to one or

OVERGROWN PEEGEE HYDRANGEA. Here form has been lost in thickening growth and flower-heads are small. *Philpott photo*

PEEGEE HYDRANGEA PRUNED. Severely cut back to a thick, branching trunk, the shrub of the previous picture will produce no flowers for a year as new shoots, breaking out from the old wood, are pinched to develop stubby new clusters of canes. The next year, buds will break from the stubs to send out long shoots with giant flower-heads. *Philpott photo*

two buds; when new growth is about 10 inches long, thin out crowded and weak shoots. Then you will have great, showy flower-heads. Where winter winds are fierce, cut off these blooms in late fall. The oakleaf, *H. quercifolia*, and the several woody lacecap species, as *H. mariesi* and *H. serrata,* and the cultivar, 'Blue Wave,' need little pruning. With a spade thin suckers that spring up away from the clump and cut out weak and crowded stems after flowering.

The beautiful pink, blue, or white hortensias, *H. macrophylla,* bloom at the tip of last year's shoots. Cut out all canes as flowers fade. *Never* tamper with new shoots. In severe climate, protect clumps over winter or the delicate terminal flower buds will be lost. Tender greenhouse cultivars of this group are suitable for garden use only where winters are very mild.

The climbing *H. petiolaris,* clinging by stem rootlets, grows well on a north wall or on large old trees. Prune out shoots that fail to cling or that have pulled away; thin vines so that the wall shows through here and there. In early spring, cut back last year's flower shoots to 1 to 2 inches; this will keep the vine tight to the wall.

HYMENOSPORUM flavum SWEETSHADE CONTINUOUS

This 30-foot tree with honey-scented flowers, tolerates neither freezing weather nor wind. You must work to get, and keep, a good specimen, but the weeks of fragrant bloom and the year-round glossy foliage make it worth while. You must pinch, pinch, pinch. The limbs tend to be few, far-between, and slender but continuous pinching from sapling to maturity builds up a sturdy, dense scaffold. Touchy about soil and exposure, as well as requiring continuous maintenance, this one is for the dedicated, expert gardener.

HYPERICUM ST.-JOHN'S-WORT EARLY SPRING

Every spring prune back shrubby kinds severely to about 1 foot or less. At the same time, cut out weak, unbranched shoots and very old stems that have become knobby. Encourage basal shoots because this woody shrub is short-lived.

IBERIS HARDY CANDYTUFT LATE SPRING

After flowers fade, shear these succulent subshrubs severely to keep them compact and healthy, and, if possible, to get a second burst of bloom. Or cut back the top part of each little mound and layer the lower branches. After these root in a few weeks, you can cut the new plants loose and transplant them in early fall.

ILEX HOLLY, BLACK-ALDER, POSSUM-HAW, WINTERBERRY ANYTIME

Young English holly, *I. aquifolium* and American *I. opaca* grow in an indeterminate mass for several years; eventually a strong leader breaks from deep within the plant, shoots up through the bush, and a typical, cone-shaped shrub develops. Don't prune young plants without leaders except to clip back out-growing shoots that look straggly. When the leader appears, leave it alone unless it grows too fast; in that case, cut it back to a reasonable length in fall. Shear well-formed hollies for the formal garden or harvest branches for Christmas from all round the plant. This encourages compact growth and avoids an unnatural look. Prune anytime but why not wait until Christmas? You may make cuts anywhere since, unlike many plants, holly produces a bud from the cambium layer regardless of where a cut is made.

Prune Chinese holly, *I. cornuta,* which grows more slowly, the same as the English and American holly. The Burford form develops into a bulky bush that you may let grow naturally or shear for a hedge. Cut back new growth hard to restrict size or, to save the berry crop, cut back the previous summer's growth in midwinter. Almost all Japanese hollies, *I. crenata,* grow as bushes, some low and spreading, others tall and upright. Prune them tight when they are moved, then cut back new growth as needed to limit size. Prune the small evergreen *I. Helleri* and *I. repandens* the same way.

Shear holly hedges or prune them tight. A sheared hedge looks formal; clip it through summer as needed to maintain a smooth surface. A tightly pruned hedge is more in keeping with today's gardens; before growth hardens, nip off most of the new growth but save the flower buds at the base of each shoot. In winter, rework the hedge with loppers to smooth it out.

Treat the deciduous black-alder, *I. verticillata*, like a border shrub. Cut out some of the oldest canes every few years and pinch basal shoots to encourage low branching. This shrub is naturally upright and tends to be bare below the crown so don't try to make it leaf out to the ground. The deciduous possum-haw, *I. decidua*, grows as a small one-trunk tree similar to hawthorn, or multiple-stemmed like a large shrub. Cut back twiggy growth as needed to keep the plant in bounds. If you pinch husky shoots as soon as they appear, you will avoid the stubs that result when you have to cut back shoots that have become woody.

Indian-bean see **CATALPA**
Irish heath see **DABOECIA**
Ironwood see **OSTRYA**

JACARANDA acutifolia SPRING

This small, open tree tolerates defoliation by a light frost but is destroyed by continuous cold. Prune saplings to a clean trunk but let permanent branches begin to develop when clearance of 8 to 10 feet is reached. Drop-prune (Chapter 2) to develop a balanced, globular head. If a limb is weighted down by a mass of foliage or flowers, thin out terminal growth by cutting back to crotches out near the ends of the limbs. Older specimens need no special pruning.

Japanese aucuba see **AUCUBA japonica**
Japanese-cedar see **CRYPTOMERIA**
Japanese clematis see **CLEMATIS**
Japanese pagoda-tree see **SOPHORA**
Japanese quince see **CHAENOMELES**
Japanese silktree see **ALBIZZIA**

JASMINUM JASMINE SPRING

Right after flowers fade, prune the oldest canes from winter jasmine, *J. nudiflorum*. Later pruning would sacrifice next year's flowers. For best results, grow this vinelike shrub on a wall trellis around a window. As flowers fade, prune the tender, shrub jasmines of southern gardens, *J. floridum*, *J. humile*, and *J. Giraldii*. Remove a few of the oldest canes if the basal crown is becoming crowded and head-back long, whippy shoots that stick up out of the plant. After it blooms, prune the tender poet's jasmine-vine, *J. officinale*, according to available space; take out weak shoots and reduce by half or more very long shoots with widely spaced leaves.

Jessamine see **CESTRUM**
Jetbead see **RHODOTYPOS**
Judas-tree see **CERCIS**

JUGLANS WALNUT, BUTTERNUT SUMMER–EARLY WINTER
Develop a straight young tree, shortening all side branches by half the year they are produced. Continue to cut off low branches as the young tree gets taller, keeping the amount of clean trunk about equal to the branch-bearing portion above until a clearance of 10 to 12 feet is reached. When the tree attains a diameter of about 3 inches, work over the top, spacing the branches on the main trunk; cut back side branches to a crotch, reducing each branch by about a third. However, the English walnut, *J. regia,* and the smaller, rather bushy butternut, *J. cinerea,* are not easy to develop into high-crowned, clean-trunked trees.

Jujube see **ZIZYPHUS**
Juniper see **JUNIPERUS**

JUNIPERUS JUNIPER, RED-CEDAR SPRING–SUMMER
Never lay a tool on a craggy, old juniper tree except to repair damage. Prune young trees freely; they even tolerate shearing, but a sheared evergreen is a ruined evergreen in most gardens. To limit the growth of all junipers—upright, vase-shaped, and spreading—cut back new growth almost all the way. Follow back along the branch to be shortened until you find a wispy little shoot that parallels the branch. Just above this, make a diagonal cut; in one summer, the shoot will replace the branch that has been removed. Be conscious of the over-all form of the juniper you are pruning and remove all branches proportionately so that the pruned shrub retains its natural, graceful, feathery appearance. With care, you can trim back a Pfitzer juniper to half its bulk without making it looked butchered. To renovate spreading plants that have gone unpruned for a few years, use loppers the first go-round, taking out several inch-thick branches way down in the plant. Finish with clippers, always pruning to a branchlet pointing the same way as the unwanted limb you cut away. To keep ground-cover

junipers short and dense, prune once each summer for several years cutting back year-old growth halfway. Older creepers need no attention except the removal of bleached looking and dead branches.

With bonsai plants, prune and train when growth starts in spring. Just before it begins to harden off, use tiny Japanese nippers to tweak out all but three or four scales of new growth. Some shoots may be removed entirely, depending on the design you want. If the plant is to be repotted, do this as growth resumes after dormancy, and shear the root ball before you replant it in the same container.

Kaki see **DIOSPYROS**

KALMIA MOUNTAIN-LAUREL, SHEEPKILL LATE SPRING–SUMMER

Remove spent blossoms by pinching off the entire cluster. To keep the tall kinds shapely, pinch back any new shoots that overgrow, but the low-growing *K. angustifolia* needs little if any pinching. When old plants get leggy, don't be afraid to cut them to the ground; new shoots will regenerate the plant in a year or two. One of the best ways to avoid crowded or lopsided growth is to cut off undesirable pieces for home decoration. If you have bees, shut them up when this shrub is blooming for the honey will be poisonous.

KALOPANAX SUMMER

Let young trees grow as they wish to develop an open, widely branched head. When they reach a diameter of 3 to 4 inches, start to remove small growth from the main branches so the main limbs will show. Drop-prune (Chapter 2) older trees from time to time to lighten the top, and take out any straight branches.

Karanda see **CARISSA**
Katsura-tree see **CERCIDIPHYLLUM**
Kentucky coffee-tree see **GYMNOCLADUS dioica**

KERRIA japonica LATE SPRING

As flowers fade, cut off worn-out and weak canes to the ground. Prune back a few other old canes to a point where new shoots are breaking out, usually about halfway down or a little nearer the base. This need not appear as a straggly, bare-legged bush crowned with a tangle of wiry, green switches that bear beautiful little golden roses.

Planted in rich soil, mulched heavily every winter with rotted barnyard manure, and properly pruned, it will grow luxuriantly, arching right to the ground, an attractive specimen or a fine informal hedge.

Kinnikinnick see **ARCTOSTAPHYLOS**

KOELREUTERIA paniculata GOLDENRAIN-TREE SUMMER

Protect the leader of young trees by pinching back tender side shoots produced below the main stalk. It is wise to let your tree choose its own form, your part being to remove crowded branches and those that cross within the scaffold of the tree. *Always prune to a crotch.* Even so, latent buds will break and make an inelegant cluster of twiggy growth; rub this off before it becomes woody. If you leave stubs, the situation is almost hopeless for developing an attractive specimen. This is one tree that I think should always be grown with three or four trunks; with no pruning whatsoever, it is the epitome of beautiful Chinese gardening. A genetic variant controls flowering; some trees bloom in spring, others of the same species late in summer. Prune tender species the same as the hardy one.

KOLKWITZIA BEAUTY-BUSH EARLY SUMMER

As flowers fade, remove a few of the oldest canes. Use a lopper and cut them to the ground. It won't be easy, because this shrub grows with canes touching, but for good health you must keep thinning them out. Leave the top alone. This reaches 12 feet and spreads 15 feet or more and *cannot* be restricted so don't plant it where space is limited.

LABURNUM GOLDENCHAIN-TREE SUMMER

These vase-shaped trees usually have a short trunk with a cluster of main limbs that lean a few degrees from perpendicular. Rub outside buds off the branches of young trees to encourage upright rather than spreading growth, and in summer pinch back green shoots that tend to grow horizontally. Old trees need no pruning; avoid cutting off large limbs because the wood does not heal well. Stake your laburnum as it has few roots and wind can rock it to death.

LAGERSTROEMIA CRAPE-MYRTLE SPRING

North of the Mason-Dixon line, prune to the ground in spring to get beautiful heads of bloom on the new wood. In the South, remove wood when it is five or six years old, thin basal shoots to keep the crown open, and pinch sappy, over-sized, summer shoots to shape the plant. If this is wood-hardy in your garden, you can grow it as a standard; prune a young plant to a single shoot and stake it. Rub off all side shoots as they appear. Grow it to a clean stalk for 6 feet or more, then cut it back and pinch new shoots until a dense ball of growth develops.

LANTANA SPRING–SUMMER

Tender where frost occurs, this may be grown as a wall shrub, garden specimen, or standard. Prostrate cultivars make good ground-covers in the Deep South. In the small garden, cut plants back to stubs at the base or on the crown of a standard. This will produce a beautiful mass of luxurious foliage and bloom. In a large garden, prune only as needed to maintain a desirable height and shape. Cut back wall shrubs hard several times during the growing period to limit outward growth and to keep them compact. In the North, grow lantana as a potted standard or as a disposable annual. As branches are produced at the top of a 3-foot standard, pinch them back to two leaves to build up a dense branching crown. Cut back hard in spring and late summer to maintain a tight, globe-shaped head. Bring indoors before frost.

Larch see **LARIX**

LARIX LARCH WINTER–LATE SPRING

Prune young trees in winter as needed to maintain a single trunk. This deciduous needle tree frequently develops one or more secondary trunks parallel to the main one; they look fine on a youngster but make an awkward mature specimen. Clean old trees of dead twigs in late spring. To limit the spread, cut back long, terminal growths on all branches. Don't injure the stubby, needle-bearing branchlets for they will not be replaced.

LAVANDULA LAVENDER SPRING–FALL

Where winters are severe, prune out dead wood as soon as it can be recognized in spring; you may have to cut back old plants hard, an unfortunate loss of flowers until late summer. Prune all plants in fall as flowers fade; shorten new growth by half. Shear hedges hard after flowering.

Lavender see **LAVANDULA**
Lavender-cotton see **SANTOLINA**
Leadplant see **AMORPHA**
Leadwortt see **PLUMBAGO capensis**
Lemon see **CITRUS**
Lemon-leaf see **GAULTHERIA**

LESPEDEZA BUSH-CLOVER EARLY SPRING
Remove dead wood and thin out the crowded mass of canes. In pruning, respect the natural form. *L. bicolor* is a twiggy upright shrub; *L. Thunbergii,* with a multiplicity of trade names, has an arching, fountain shape. In the North, both freeze to the ground; cut them back in early spring before new shoots come up from the base. Avoid summer pruning which reduces the crop of fall flowers and ruins the form of *L. Thunbergii* (Sometimes this is mistakenly called *Desmodium.*)

LEUCOTHOË Catesbaei DROOPING LEUCOTHOË SPRING
You will have little need to prune either evergreen or deciduous species. Just cut out dead twigs in spring and pinch back new shoots to shape the plant. If a very old trunk is failing, cut it to the ground.

LIGUSTRUM PRIVET WINTER–SPRING–SUMMER
On unsheared border specimens, cut out at the base about a fourth of the oldest wood every four years in winter. Remove weak basal shoots and pinch new growth as needed to shape the bush through the summer. Allow most species 6 feet of space and they will grow about that tall. Some get larger. Shear hedges through the summer when they look ragged. Slope the sides toward the top so that light will reach the lower branches on both sides. Cut back newly set hedge plants halfway or more, and shear them frequently and hard for two or three years to build up a broad dense base; allow no more than 6 inches of growth through a growing season. In early spring, renew old hedges by cutting them back to 1 foot or less. Then they will need plenty of fertilizer and water through the next summer. Tender evergreen species grown as unsheared specimens may need heavy pruning every other winter to keep them neat and full.

Lilac see **SYRINGA**

Lily-of-the-valley-tree see **CLETHRA**
Lime see **CITRUS** or **TILIA**
Linden see **TILIA**

LINDERA SPICE-BUSH, BENZOIN WINTER

These are best left unpruned until they become old and oversized. Then cut to the ground to make them renew from the basal crown. Thin and shape as needed by cutting to a crotch when the bush is completely dormant; you can bring the cut branches inside to force the little, yellow flower clusters. This shrub seems to look well-groomed even if you never touch it.

LIQUIDAMBAR Styraciflua SWEET-GUM-TREE SUMMER

Remove crowded branches while they are small and head-back over-reaching limbs by pinching off the tips to avoid heavy pruning later. While trees are small, take off a few longer branches each year for clearance. This tree does not heal well. Though somewhat gangling in youth, your sweet gum will mature into a portly, well-furnished gentleman with almost no pruning.

LIRIODENDRON Tulipifera TULIP-TREE, TULIP-POPLAR EARLY SUMMER

This tall, stately tree with perfect form needs no pruning, but it requires deep, rich, moist soil for proper growth. Otherwise it develops dead branches through the top, and side branches complete with the leader. Annual pruning plus good culture soon correct these difficulties. Seal broken limbs immediately with tree paint and, if the trunk sunscalds or winterburns, use a sharp, heavy knife to cut out the dry, sunken bark; trace back to live bark and paint the exposed wood with tree-wound dressing. If you live where ice storms and heavy winds are common, forego the tulip-tree as it is extremely brittle.

Locust see **ROBINIA**
Loganberries see **RUBUS**

LONICERA HONEYSUCKLE WINTER–SUMMER

Cut back to half its length each shoot of a newly set *bush* so it will develop a dense inner structure. Don't try to limit spread or height by pruning because you will destroy the graceful form. Species range from waist-high to 15 feet; try to find the one that fits your spot. Leave unpruned or cut out some of the oldest wood at the ground every four or five years. Hundred-year-old plants with massive inner trunks bloom just about as freely as renewed ones. Semi-evergreen sorts, as *L. fragrantissima,* need more renovation than deciduous species.

Prune hardy honeysuckle *vines* according to their nature and your use; cultivars like 'Goldflame' are well-behaved and training is more important than pruning. Japanese honeysuckle, *L. japonica,* is an example of a rampant sort that must be trimmed severely to keep it in bounds. Remove gnarled, diseased, and badly entwined old wood in winter; pinch summer shoots to encourage branching. On banks, you can mow or shear plants; in the garden, watch out for ground runners that sneak along for yards before reaching up to strangle your best viburnum or some other treasure.

Loquat see **ERIOBOTRYA japonica**

LYCIUM MATRIMONY-VINE, BOX-THORN WINTER–SUMMER

Prune these rambling shrubs in winter to tidy them; remove sprawling, trailing branches and stubby, twiggy, old canes. Use a spade to dig out rooted tips and suckers. If you must grow this, it is best to train it as a wall shrub. Keep it tied flat to a trellis and whack off any branches that reach out. Pinch new growth hard in summer.

LYCOPERSICUM TOMATO SUMMER

There are many ways of training and pruning tomato plants. First, consider the classification of the kind you are growing. Most early tomatoes, especially commercial types, are "determinate," that is, they produce a single, heavy crop that ripens almost all at once, and then the vines are through bearing. These sorts are best left unpruned and unstaked. Where mud is a problem, put down a deep bed of straw before the plants begin to sprawl, and let it go at that.

Home-garden varieties are "indeterminate," that is, they produce cluster after cluster. While fruit is ripening low on the plant, flowers are still coming on up near the top. These are the plants that need to be staked. Allow just one stem to develop. A side branch, called a "sucker" will develop where each leaf joins the main stem. Pinch this out as soon as it appears unless it comes from immediately *below* a flower cluster; in that case, let the sucker develop two leaves, then

STAKED TOMATO PLANT. Indeterminate types of tomatoes are best staked and then pinched as shown. Remove all suckers as they form in leaf crotches *except* those immediately below a fruit cluster as at A. Let these suckers make a pair of leaves, then pinch them at B to check further development. The extra foliage on the stopped suckers makes food that feeds directly into the developing fruit. This method of pruning originated from research by the late Dr. C. M. Tucker at the University of Missouri.

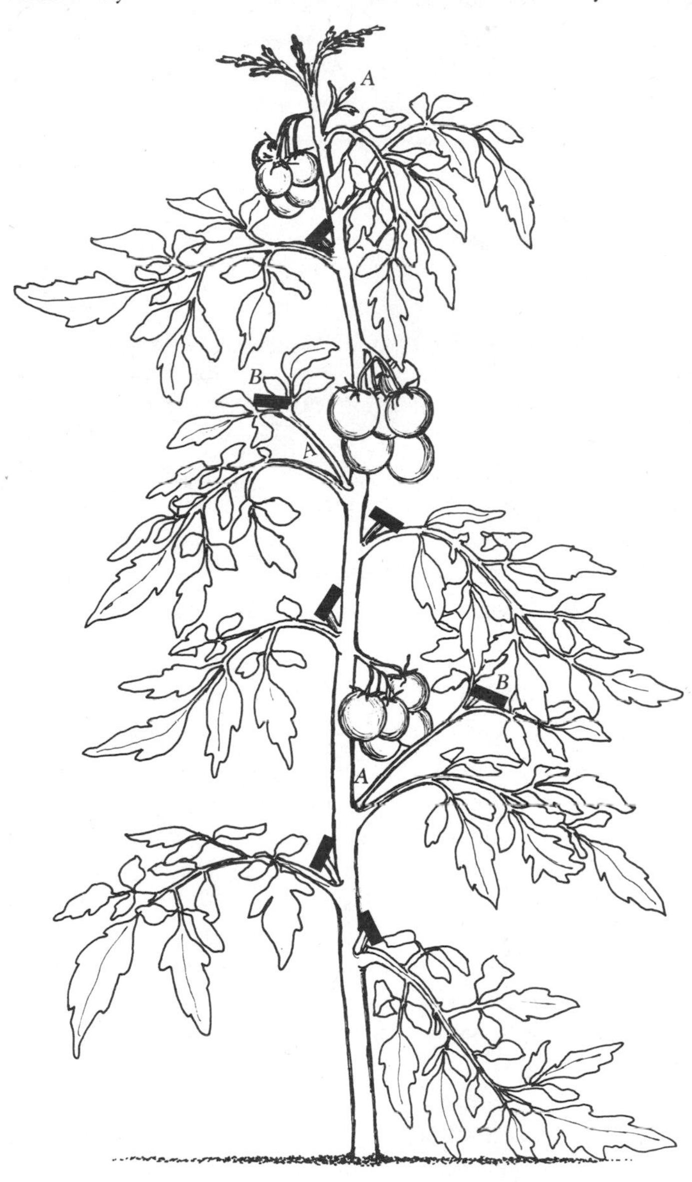

pinch it. This extra foliage just below a flower cluster manufactures a lot of food that is carried directly up into the ripening fruits. If the sucker is allowed to become a complete branch, the main stem loses a proportionate amount of water and nourishment. Some gardeners like to let the lowest sucker on the plant develop into a secondary trunk for late fruit. You may try both methods and see which works better for you. There is great variation in behavior among tomatoes, so use the pinching technique that gives you the best and biggest crop for your table.

MACLURA pomifera OSAGE-ORANGE WINTER

Grow only the male form. On young trees no pruning is needed; remove crowded branches from older specimens. Nothing can be done about the bright orange surface roots that mar the garden for yards round the tree. For bullproof hedges, plant rooted whips a foot apart and cut them almost to the ground. Bend over the vigorous new shoots the next winter and twist them into adjacent ones to form a barbed entanglement. Every winter, cut off twiggy side branches and braid the long, unbranched, thorny ones into the hedge. This was the original "barbed wire" farm enclosure of the Midwest.

Madagascar-jasmine see **STEPHANOTIS**
Madrona see **ARBUTUS**

MAGNOLIA BULL-BAY, CUCUMBER-TREE, SWEETBAY, YULAN SUMMER

Prune in summer only; *never* take off wood large enough to need a saw; magnolias do not heal well. You may prune out small, crowding branches with a lopper but it is better to control your tree by pinching new shoots. Some kinds, particularly large-flowered, deciduous types like *M. Soulangeana,* respond well to the weighting of branches, a technique that spreads the crown and shapes the tree without pruning. You can train the evergreen bull-bay against a wall; start with a young tree and remove all branches except those that parallel the wall. Tie these out flat and pinch tips. Save only the new shoots that grow flat and pinch these back when three or four leaves are produced.

MAHONIA OREGON-GRAPE, OREGON-HOLLY SUMMER

Cut out old branches that are bare below and broomy at the tip.

With a spade, cut out basal sprouts if a clump gets too large. Cut back newly set bushes for they are slow to establish. Clip creeping species close when young to thicken up clumps.

Maidenhair-tree see **GINKGO**
Mallow see **HIBISCUS**

MALUS APPLE WINTER–SUMMER

Winter pruning produces vigorous growth in spring; summer pruning restricts growth. Pruning for fruit is usually done through the winter; pruning that requires a saw must be done during the dormant period. The Lorette system (Chapter 2) suitable for dwarf and espalier-trained trees, is restricted to summer.

Prune young apple trees to a modified leader scaffold or to a central-leader scaffold. Except for notably upright varieties, like 'McIntosh', and 'Early Transparent', the central-leader scaffold is more satisfactory. Prune a young tree to four lateral or side branches with wide crotches that face in different directions and are 6 to 8 inches apart on the trunk. The lowest branch should be about 2 feet above the ground. Maintain a clean leader above these laterals for one year, and shorten the laterals to equal length. No more pruning is required until a tree begins to bear. Then head-back laterals to keep the leader dominant, take out growth pointing inward, and also remove weak inside branches. After the first crop is harvested, cut back all laterals a little. Older, heavier methods of pruning produce very large apples, but few of them, and the trees are unsightly. Try to limit your pruning to removal of crowded and weak young wood.

Espalier-trained apple trees are pruned through the summer. For best results, nip back new growths to two or three leaves when it is pencil-sized and has become slightly woody. Rub off undesirable side branches while they are still tender.

CRABAPPLE SUMMER

Flowering crabapples vary in form from the bushy white *M. Sargentii* and weeping 'Red Jade' to very tall upright forms like *M. Zumi calocarpa*. Remove only weak internal shoots and crowded branches, always cutting to a crotch. Or remove a few branches at the trunk taking care to leave no stubs to mar the beauty of the tree or admit decay. Sometimes old trees become so massive they lose form entirely. After they bloom you can strategically remove up to a third of the branches next the trunk and thin out the remaining ones as well. Be sure to cover cuts with tree paint. Thin out weeping and spreading forms to feature their distinctive patterns of growth. Columnar and

APPLE-TREE FIRST PRUNING. (opposite, lower) Right after planting, interfering and crowded branches are removed where they originate. All remaining side branches are shortened to about the same length. *Roche photo*

APPLE-TREE SECOND PRUNING. (opposite, upper) To develop a tree with a modified leader, the center stem is left somewhat longer than the side branches. *Roche photo*

PRUNING FOR EFFECT. This ancient apple tree is a handsome feature. Pruned for beauty, not fruit, its value lies in its canopy of spring bloom and the open shade it affords a flower border below. The top is thinned yearly and the trunks kept free of suckers and sprouts. Before you pull out a tired misshapen old fruit tree, consider its possibility as an arresting garden accent; careful pruning can make the most of gnarled and twisted limbs. *Miner photo*

narrowly upright types can be further narrowed by removing branches growing outward.

Manzanita see **ARCTOSTAPHYLOS**
Maple see **ACER**
Matrimony-vine see **LYCIUM**

MELALEUCA linariifolia SNOW-IN-SUMMER FALL

Prune this white-flowering tropical tree as flowers fade; thin overly dense parts of the crown by drop-pruning (Chapter 2) and remove lower limbs at the trunk as needed for clearance. Your young tree will be narrowly upright; in maturity it will open out to form a round-headed crown. Shrubby and small tree-form species, sometimes called "bottle-brush," need considerable thinning as they become twiggy and dense; avoid leaving stubs for branches do not grow out from cut-back sections.

MELIA CHINABERRY-TREE, BEAD-TREE SUMMER

This twiggy, tight-headed tree needs little thinning. It grows like an umbrella catalpa—a pole with a ball of green on the top. While young, it requires tight pruning to build up a dense head. It is well suited to its Oklahoma use—shading the chicken yard.

Mexican–orange see **CHOISYA ternata**
Mezeron see **DAPHNE**
Mimosa see **ALBIZZIA**
Mock-orange see **PHILADELPHUS**
Monkey-puzzle tree see **ARAUCARIA**
Monkshood-vine see **AMPELOPSIS**

MORUS MULBERRY WINTER–SUMMER

Develop the leader of a young tree intended for shade by removing side shoots for 2 to 3 feet below the tip while growth is dormant. Later, thin the branches to develop an open-headed tree. Or grow with multiple trunks and space branches far enough apart to give character. Weeping trees are usually left unpruned though some thinning of new shoots in summer is desirable. For a hedge, plant whips a foot apart and cut to 6 inches; through summer, clip back new growth every few weeks to gradually build up dense, twiggy growth that may reach to 12 feet.

Mountain-ash see **SORBUS**
Mountain-laurel see **KALMIA**

MUHLENBECKIA WIRE-PLANT SUMMER

These tangled little subshrubs, half vine and half bush, are best used as ground-covers. At planting time, clip back to a whisk broom. Afterwards cut out winter-killed wood and any branches that stick up, destroying symmetry.

Mulberry see **MORUS**

MYRICA BAYBERRY, WAX-MYRTLE, SWEET-GALE WINTER

Cut back newly planted bushes hard as they are difficult to establish; wintertime is best. The tall species, *M. cerifera* and *M. californica* (tender), are effective pruned as small, three- to five-stemmed trees with clusters of foliage here and there along the trunks. Low kinds need pruning only to remove dead canes each year. Sweet-gale spreads by suckers; cut these out with a sharp spade to limit growth. Scottish folk use sweet-gale leaves, symbol of the Campbell clan, instead of hops in their beer and also in the clothes chest to impart a sweet odor.

Myrtle see **MYRTUS**

MYRTUS MYRTLE CONTINUOUS

An ancient plant, the true myrtle adapts itself to your whims so long as your garden is frost-free. You may shear it into a hedge or a topiary, or train it to a geometric pattern on a wall. You may also grow it loose and open as a shrub, building an internal structure of well-spaced main branches to bear the leaf load. Don't cut back a specimen plant from the outside, but reach in and take out part of a main branch that droops from the weight of foliage or, getting too tall, spoils the symmetry of growth. Dwarf forms need no pruning.

NANDINA HEAVENLY-BAMBOO SUMMER

Leave it alone, and it will grow to stately heights (south) or make a rude bunch (north). But it is better to take out one or two of the oldest inside canes at the ground each summer. For the Japanese garden, thin the plant to just a few, widely spaced canes of various heights. *Never* cut back a cane part way.

Nannybush see **VIBURNUM**
Natal-plum see **CARISSA**

NERIUM OLEANDER SUMMER

As flowers fade, cut back last year's growth by two-thirds or more. To encourage branching, pinch new shoots when they have four or five leaves. Renew garden shrubs (south) every six to eight years by cutting out a few of the very oldest canes at the ground. Or grow as a standard: Rub off developing side buds from a staked plant until it is 5 feet or taller; then pinch out the terminal bud; allow only side buds at the tip to develop and cut foot-long shoots back to two leaves to build up a dense head. Every year, after flowering, cut these back hard.

New-Jersey-tea see **CEANOTHUS**
Ninebark see **PHYSOCARPUS**
Norfolk island-pine see **ARAUCARIA**

NOTHOFAGUS ANTARCTIC-BEECH WINTER

While it is small, prune this tender evergreen (south) or deciduous hardwood tree (north) to a single leader. Space the growth of well-developed young trees (4 to 6-inch diameter trunks) by sawing out crowded and poorly formed branches. Mature trees require only maintenance pruning.

NYSSA SOUR GUM, BLACK GUM, TUPELO WINTER

Prune young trees, which are indeterminate and twiggy, to a clean leader. Reduce side branches to half and remove all side branchlets on the year-old leader. Or allow the tree to grow in natural form; for about forty years, it will be small and twiggy; then it will grow upright, lower branches will be shaded out, and eventually it will become a tall specimen with a high diffuse crown. Trees past the sapling stage need no pruning except the removal of crowded branches and dead branchlets.

Oak see **QUERCUS**
Old-man's-beard see **CHIONANTHUS**

OLEA europaea OLIVE EARLY SPRING

For shade, let your tree go its own way, only head-back one side of a V-crotch if it forms, remove any crowded or weak branches, and enough lower limbs to allow plenty of headroom. As this is a slow grower and not inclined to be troublesome, it needs only a minimum of maintenance pruning. It will bear a crop of rather small olives about every second year.

For fruit, begin training early, either on the open-center or modified-leader system. For the open center, remove the leader of a young tree and save four or five well-spaced side branches, the lowest about 3 feet from the ground in an orchard, 5 to 6 feet on the lawn. Head-back scaffold branches to uniform length. Each year, thin out last year's side branches to build up a well-balanced, goblet-shaped tree.

For a modified-leader tree, remove all but three well-spaced side branches and the upper third of the leader. The next year (or it may take two years), let three or four more well-spaced side branches develop along the central leader. Then cut out the leader immediately above the uppermost branch. This branch will gradually grow to replace the leader, but the tree will have lost its vertical tendency and will develop a globe-shaped crown. As with an open-center tree, head-back young scaffold branches and thin out any side branches on them so wood will be well spaced and open. For an annual crop of large olives on bearing trees, cut out about half of the previous year's fruiting wood.

Two problems will plague you for fifty years or so! Sprouts will break from the basal crown and suckers appear on trunk and main scaffold limbs. Suppress these ruthlessly! Pull the basal suckers the moment they appear; every day is critical, for, as they grow they develop a basal cluster of latent buds that breaks to form lots more sprouts when you cut back the mother sprout. Don't let water sprouts reach the "shoot" stage. With a gloved hand, rub off burgeoning buds on trunk and limbs. If your tree seems overly inclined toward sprouting, ease up on fertilizer and stop top pruning for two to three years. Heavy top work always results in suckers and water sprouts.

Oleander see **NERIUM**
Oleaster see **ELAEAGNUS**
Olive see **OLEA europaea**
Orange see **CITRUS**
Oregon-grape see **MAHONIA**
Oregon-holly see **MAHONIA**
Osage-orange see **MACLURA pomifera**

OSMANTHUS HOLLY-OLIVE EARLY SPRING–SUMMER
To keep mature shrubs compact and symmetrical, cut back last year's growth early in spring. On young plants, pinch out new growth in spring to force the development of a leader. Shear hedges just before growth resumes in spring, and once or twice more through summer.

OSTRYA HOP-HORNBEAM, IRONWOOD WINTER
Cut back halfway the side branches of seedlings and young trees; remove shoots that compete with the leader. Grow trees unpruned as small, straight-trunked specimens or with multiple trunks. Then thin out branches so trunks show through the head of the tree. American hop-hornbeam, *O. virginiana,* may be thinned and pruned for a picturesque, gnarled effect. The European *O. carpinifolia* and Japanese *O. japonica* look best as straight, single-trunked specimens.

OXYDENDRUM arboreum SORREL-TREE, SOURWOOD SUMMER
Soaring to 80 feet in its Appalachian habitat, in the garden this handsome tree usually stays small, irregular, and picturesque. Leave it unpruned or remove a branch here and there to emphasize character. Plant it for dappled shade and height above azaleas and rhododendrons; thin the top so sunlight comes through and prune up to a shallow layer of branches supported by a twisted trunk kept clean of side shoots. Don't clip off spent clusters of flower spikes for they have brilliant autumn color.

PACHISTIMA RAT-STRIPPER SUMMER
Shear newly set plants; clip over established plants to nip off straggly shoots and old, inside branches that have died out. Bury low-lying stems around the edge of the clumps, letting tips stick up; these will take root and increase your stock. If you live on neutral or limey soil

or north of Zone 4, you will have to prune more because of winterkill and dieback.

PAEONIA PEONY SPRING–SUMMER–FALL

Cut herbaceous peonies to the ground late in summer or early fall as leaves mature and look dry. Don't wait for frost to knock down the tops. Burn the stalks to avoid disease. On woody tree peonies prune out winter-injured shoots as leaf buds open in spring; very old clumps must be thinned, a painful necessity but necessary for best appearance. Keep two or three very old canes of various heights and one or two young canes; cut out the rest in midsummer. Save all side branches; your old bushes should appear rather columnar with gnarled trunks bearing great swatches of foliage and showy blooms.

Paper-mulberry see **BROUSSONETIA**
Parasol-pine see **SCIADOPITYS verticillata**

PARTHENOCISSUS VIRGINIA-CREEPER, BOSTON-IVY WINTER–SUMMER

Prune freely when vines overgrow; cut out pieces that have pulled loose from supports and remove any tag ends that hang loose; prune and train to one layer. Cut back before growth reaches woodwork and window screens because the disc-shaped holdfasts leave permanent marks once they fasten on. Very old vines do not renew well if cut back; it is better to start young replacements before stripping down an ancient plant.

PASSIFLORA PASSION-FLOWER CONTINUOUS

Prune these vines as needed to keep them within limits, but remember that summer pruning removes flowering wood. Some kinds are rampant; when growth has ceased, cut these back rather severely, perhaps to just one main stem with a few short branches. Let more delicate kinds run at will, but train the vines over the supports rather than allowing them to form a ropy tangle. If frost injuries your plant, cut it back severely. New growth may break from the old stem or from the crown. Semihardy kinds, grown as far north as Kansas City, freeze to the ground in winter but come up from the root very late in spring to bloom by midsummer. Injured plants may throw a heavy crop of root suckers that break out for yards around. Pull rather than spade these out. You may grow the vines in pots, pruning them heavily for a season or two to develop a short, stocky "trunk" with heavy, spurlike branches. Plants must be wintered indoors. These flower beautifully in midsummer heat.

PAULOWNIA EMPRESS-TREE EARLY SPRING–SUMMER

These "punky" trees require heavy pruning when young to develop a single trunk with a definite leader. Cut out basal shoots as they appear; cut back hard any side branches that tend to dominate the leader; through the summer, pinch back all side shoots until the tree is well shaped. In early spring, cut out winter-injured branch ends. Old trees, cut to the ground, sometimes grow again with multiple trunks.

Pawpaw see **ASIMINA triloba**
Peach see **PRUNUS Persica**
Pear see **PYRUS**
Pearl-bush see **EXOCHORDA**
Pecan see **CARYA**
Peegee see **HYDRANGEA**
Peony see **PAEONIA**
Pepper-vine see **AMPELOPSIS**

PERNETTYA mucronata EARLY SPRING–FALL

Prune back these rather tender little evergreen shrubs in early spring if they have grown too open and loose. Otherwise, let them alone. Late in fall, cut short sprays of the colorful berries to further shape mature plants and control height.

PERSEA americana AVOCADO SPRING

Planted in a frost-free garden, seedling avocados may grow to 50 feet or more; budded trees are much less vigorous. Plant your young tree with care to avoid root injury; then pinch out the tip to encourage side branching. Through the next few years, build a low, round head of well-spaced limbs by cutting out pencil-sized branches that grow inward or that are poorly spaced. Pinch off strong shoots that break beyond the crown of a plant. Older trees only require the removal of weak or interfering branches. *Always dab warm grafting wax or tree-wound dressing on fresh cuts, even small ones, as avocado wood is extremely subject to decay.* Pinch out your potted seedling when it has five or six leaves; at the same time, feed it with diluted fish emulsion. Thereafter, pinch new shoots when they have four or five leaves. If you supply a well-drained soil mixture and repot each spring, your plant can be kept going for several years, though chances are it will never reach the point of flowering.

Persimmon see **DIOSPYROS**

PETREA QUEEN'S CREEPER, PURPLE-WREATH SPRING

These twining vines grow outdoors in the Deep South but in a greenhouse in areas where frosts occur. They twine tight and are trained with a single stem on each vertical support. In February, head-back the main shoots as needed and shorten side branches to accommodate the available space. If necessary, they may be cut to two or three leaves. Also remove weak, dangling tags of vine and cut away weak, basal shoots. Don't try this as a pot plant for, so confined, it will not flower; it requires a spacious root run and considerable mature wood.

PHELLODENDRON CORK-TREE SUMMER

Prune seedlings and whips to a single trunk; rub off burgeoning side buds before they make shoots; if a shoot appears, clip it off right at the trunk. Let saplings of 2-inch diameter develop side branches but shorten these, especially near the leader, to keep the tree going straight. An alternative is to cut year-old seedlings to the ground; then grow as multiple-trunked specimens; only a little pruning of side branches will be needed.

PHILADELPHUS MOCK-ORANGE (not syringa) SPRING–SUMMER–FALL

Leave the large, leggy *P. coronarius* and *P. virginalis* unpruned, except to remove a few of the oldest canes every third or fourth year in early spring or fall. This will open up a crowded base. In the same way, on the smaller arching kinds cut out a few crowding canes at the ground-line, and thin out twiggy inside wood by cutting back some growth to a crotch or to a main branch. Don't cut back ends of branches or you will get an ugly, broom-shaped shrub. When new basal shoots of both tall and arching growers are a few inches high, pinch out tips and continue to do this through summer. These mostly

6- to 8-foot shrubs (except for the newer dwarfs) need space, at least a 5-foot spread, so don't rely on pruning to restrict them to small quarters.

PHOTINIA CHRISTMAS-BERRY LATE SPRING

Shorten vigorous shoots to keep your shrub well shaped. Pinch back several times any soft shoots produced from the basal crown or on low branches. Do this through the growing season to encourage low branching. Cut out old deteriorating wood and crowded branches at the base or at a crotch. Prune as little as possible. You may grow *P. villosa* (*arbutifolia*) and the tender *P. serrulata* as small, single-trunked trees that need only thinning and a little drop-pruning (Chapter 2) to limit height.

PHYLLOSTACHYS BAMBOO EARLY SPRING

Remove at the ground old canes showing deterioration at the tip; thin out crowded canes and use a sharp spade to cut back creeping underground stems reaching beyond the clump. Avoid cutting back a cane part way for it will not resume growth and looks awful. After pruning, keep your grove beautiful by washing canes and foliage with a strong stream of water. Then loosen the soil and mulch with a mixture of well-rotted stable manure and sand.

PHYSOCARPUS NINEBARK SUMMER

Prune according to the need of the particular species you are growing. If your shrub is nicely shaped and arching, it will require little attention; from time to time, prune out some of the oldest canes at the ground and thin twiggy branches inside the shrub, cutting to a crotch. If your shrub grows upright and ragged, it will take more maintenance; remove a third of the oldest wood every three years; thin broomy branches by taking out inside twigs at a crotch, and pinch out basal shoots through summer to encourage low branching. Avoid pruning back the ends of outer canes as they then become very brushy.

PICEA SPRUCE SPRING–MIDSUMMER

Prune as little as possible. In spring, you may clip soft new shoots to half their length all over the tree to shape and retard growth but use a fine clipper on one shoot at a time; don't use hedge shears. In midsummer, remove any smaller trunk that may show up inside to compete with the main trunk; reach in and cut it out where it originates. Growth will be sparse on that side for a year or two but will eventually thicken up by itself.

PIERIS ANDROMEDA SUMMER

Pinch new shoots to thicken up an open specimen, and nip out spent flower spikes before seed forms to weaken the plant. Cut back any cankered branches immediately to healthy, undiscolored wood; disinfect your clippers between cuts. If your old plant declines and dieback is persistent, replace it; renewal is almost impossible.

Pigeon-berry see **DURANTA**
Pine see **PINUS**

PINUS PINE SPRING

Cut "candles" on side branches of young trees to half or less after needles have expanded but before growth has hardened. You may use the hedge shears on young Austrian, Ponderosa, Scotch, and white pines for three or four years to keep them symmetrical and dense, but hand-work young Japanese red, black, and white pines for they grow diffuse and open. If you want a "character" specimen, forego formal shaping; let the tree grow as it will, but protect the leader by pinching out branches that compete with it. In time, remove branches here and there to expose the trunk; if you wish, stop-back candles on side branches and top so that the tree appears ancient and windswept. You can thicken and retard older pines by reducing by a third the length of candles at the tree tip and branch ends, and the surrounding ones by half or more. Remove secondary leaders at their point of origin as they appear; never remove a lower branch for it will not be replaced. Shear young spreading types, as Mugho and stone, for a few years; then pinch back selected new growth to keep plants compact but not symmetrical.

Prune pines grown as bonsai when new growth expands; use a fine nipper to remove most of the new growth without injuring the few needles that are left. Cut back older branches at the same time; shear roots at replanting time and just before resumption of growth.

PITTOSPORUM CONTINUOUS

Most of these need little pruning; the trunks of tree-forms have to be raised by removing lower branches from time to time for clearance and some may develop suckers on trunks and large branches that you will want to rub off. The narrowly upright shrub types require no pruning, but you can thin the branches, exposing trunks here and there for an interesting pattern. Low, spreading kinds need a little pruning from time to time throughout the year. They tend to send out long shoots from just below the terminal leaf clusters and these interrupt the dense, undulating mass of the plant. Cut them out as they appear. Tender where frost occurs, these are valuable tub plants in the North where their handsome foliage rather than the fragrant flowers become a garden feature. If a variegated pittosporum throws an all-green branch, cut it out before it overgrows the less vigorous variegated branches.

PLATANUS SYCAMORE, PLANE-TREE SUMMER–WINTER
Prune newly set whips hard; remove all side shoots at end of summer until growth reaches 6 feet. Head-back side branches on saplings to encourage a straight, dominant leader. Clear side branches from about the lower third of the trunk; remove more branches as the tree grows taller. Old trees require only maintenance pruning; don't be concerned about heavy, wide-spread limbs; they won't drop although they look mighty precarious. If you wish to pleach your trees (Chapter 2), that is, prune and train them so they are flat, spread out, and whacked back at the top, winter is the time; then cut back the new growth in early summer. However I hope you won't engage in this torturous technique that should have gone with the Inquisition.

Plum see **PRUNUS**

PLUMBAGO capensis CAPE-PLUMBAGO, LEADWORT WINTER
Cut out all old wood that is without leaves and non-flowering; then energy will go to young vigorous shoots. Shortly after such pruning, you will have twice the number of flower-heads and they will be large. Young plants are easy to keep in good shape if you thin them well at least once each year. Whack older plants to the ground; they will look rough for a time, but will recover in the next growing season. Or you may take out about a third of the oldest wood, head-back the whippy young shoots, and count on two to three years to transform a brushy, ill-kept specimen into a beautiful shrub. When frost blackens the tips, cut off the injured wood well back into green tissue; new shoots will soon conceal the damage.

Plum-yew see **CEPHALOTAXUS**

PODOCARPUS SUMMER
Pinch back repeatedly or shear seedlings and rooted cuttings to develop dense, bushy plants. Older specimens grown in tubs or in the garden require little pruning though you may wish to reduce new growth by half to keep plants compact. Shear hedges if they look ragged. Root-prune older plants all round before transplanting.

Poinsettia see **EUPHORBIA pulcherrima**

PONCIRUS trifoliata HARDY-ORANGE EARLY SPRING–SUMMER
Prune back to just a few leaves any strong shoots that disturb symmetry. Little other pruning is required but you can thin these graceful little trees to feature the handsome branching habit. Grown in a formal hedge, they may be sheared once or twice through summer or, for a less formal hedge, you may prune them tight in early spring, cutting to a crotch each time. For a wall shrub, begin with a single-trunk specimen and fan out the branches in an informal pattern; thin out the leafy wood so the wall shows through.

Pond-cypress see **TAXODIUM**

POPULUS POPLAR, ASPEN, COTTONWOOD, ABELE SPRING–SUMMER
Cut back newly set whips of columnar poplars to a foot to make them branch heavily from the base. Then, every spring for a few years cut new growth to half while it is soft and green. Trees look best branched from the ground up rather than with several feet of bare trunk in the Italian or Swiss style. For a "Normandy" look, thin out branches severely, leaving only an occasional cluster of leaf-bearing stubs on a clean, tall trunk.

Prune quaking aspens as *P. tremuloides*, only to protect the leader on young plants. You may thin the branches in a clump but drop-prune (Chapter 2) to avoid stubs, and work carefully so as not to scar the fragile bark. Paint wounds immediately and reseal them a year later.

Strip all side branches from whips of the cottonwoods, as the northern *P. deltoides* and *P. Sargentii* of the Great Plains, until trees are 8 to 10 feet tall. Then let branches develop well below the leader, but cut them back halfway for one growing season. Keep the leader free of side shoots for a few more years. Old cottonwoods require only maintenance pruning; if the top become dangerously heavy and widespread, resort to drop-pruning. Avoid stubbing back big branches, "early-settler" style.

Grow the white poplar or abele *P. alba* in open groves. To avoid black scar tissue on the silvery bark, clean the trunks to 12 feet or more while the branches are quite small. These trees require little maintenance pruning but look better if thinned every ten years or so. Avoid heavy pruning and any root injury so you won't have to cope with a great crop of wide-ranging root sprouts. If these appear, spade them out or, better, poison them with very dilute brush-killer so the bud cluster on the root is destroyed.

Possum-haw see **ILEX**

POTENTILLA CINQUEFOIL EARLY SPRING–MIDSUMMER

Nip winter-killed wood from the shrubs when buds swell enough to indicate area of damage; don't overprune in spring or you will reduce bloom in August when other flowers are scarce. After the first heavy flush of flowers, tidy up the shrubs by thinning crowded branchlets and cut back leggy shoots. Some species and cultivars make dandy little hedges; shear these in summer.

Prickly-ash see **ZANTHOXYLUM**
Privet see **LIGUSTRUM**

PRUNUS SWEET AND SOUR CHERRIES SUMMER–WINTER

Prune sweet Hart cherries (*P. avium Juliana* cultivars), and the sweet, hard-fleshed Bigarreaus (*P. avium duracina* cultivars), also the sour cherries (*P. Cerasus* cultivars, as 'Early Richmond' and 'Montmorency'), to a modified leader scaffold. At planting time, retain three or four well-placed, wide-crotched side or lateral branches as a start for the scaffold, with the lowest branch about 18 inches from the ground, the others about 6 inches apart and spaced round the tree. Remove other branches to the trunk but keep the leader intact. Cut back the laterals to about the length of the shortest one.

In the home garden, balance the leaf load on each lateral by nipping off excessive shoots in June; this helps all the laterals to grow at the

PRUNING A YOUNG FRUIT TREE. When trees come into bearing, weak, ingrowing, and crowded limbs must be removed. To get a clean cut, use a heavy lopper for any wood over finger-thickness. Position the tool so the cutting blade, not the holding blade, is next to the trunk; in this way you leave a minimum of stub. *Flower & Garden photo*

same rate. For two or three years—until the tree has six or seven nicely spaced, wide-crotched branches—keep one or two more well-spaced laterals coming out from the growing leader. Then cut off the leader just above the highest lateral branch. This will develop into a modified leader once the true leader has been removed.

Now you are finished with the job of building a strong, well-branched, modified leader scaffold, and no more pruning is required until the tree begins to fruit. Sour cherries are seldom pruned except to cut out dead, weak, or rubbing branches. With sweet cherry trees, take a saw to the tops when these begin to grow too high. Cut out the leader just above a cluster of three or four laterals; take care to leave no stub. A tree pruned this way is hardly a thing of beauty but it *is* fruitful and you *can* reach the cherries. Of course, you can decide to forego fruit and let your sweet cherry grow on to a large, handsome shade tree.

WILD CHERRY SUMMER

These ornamental native trees with pendant clusters of small, white flowers followed by dangling clusters of tiny dark red or black cherries need little pruning. Protect the leader on saplings and thin growth on young trees to develop a sturdy, branching system. Cut back half of each narrow V-crotch while it is young. For lawn use, as the tree grows, trim up the lower branches to a clearance of 10 feet or more. Burn all cut or fallen leafy branches; wilted foliage becomes *extremely poisonous.* Included here are the sweet wild cherry, the mazzard or gean (*P. avium*), European bird cherry (*P. Padus*), wild red cherry (*P. pensylvanica*), and the wild black cherry (*P. serotina*).

WILD PLUM SUMMER–WINTER

Growing as small trees with rough-barked, gnarled trunks that carry a low crown of tightly branched limbs, American plums, their cultivars and hybrids, form thickets by root sprouts. Prune young trees to a central leader scaffold—no easy job, this—save three low branches with wide crotches that are about 8 inches apart and well spaced around the trunk. Also preserve the leader. Through the next one or two summers, save about three more branches to complete the scaffold. Strip all side branches from the scaffold branches for at least 18 inches from the trunk. Drop-prune (Chapter 2) the scaffold branches to keep them of even length until fruit production starts; then head them all back to encourage end branching. Try to build up a rather open half-round crown. As root sprouts appear, cut them out with a long, narrow spade or "sharpshooter" or poison them with very dilute brush-killer, but do not use brush-killing chemicals on sprouts within the drip-line of the tree. Included here are the American plum (*P. americana*), Chickasaw plum (*P. angustifolia*), wild goose plum (*P. Munsoniana*), and Oklahoma plum (*P. gracilis*).

FLOWERING CHERRY, FLOWERING APRICOT WINTER

These ornamentals are pruned the same way. Prune standard trees very little; just remove enough branches while trees are young to develop a fairly open, central-leader type of growth; clean the main scaffold limbs of side branches for 2 feet or more from the trunk. Always drop-prune (Chapter 2) the crown when wood has to be removed to lighten it. The Higan cherries are rough, twiggy little trees that are improved by rather hard thinning when the trunk diameter measures 3 to 4 inches. The Mume needs almost no pruning after the scaffold is developed. Many of the flowering cherries have special forms, as the columnar 'Amanogawa' or the weeping, autumn-flowering 'Higan'. Prune these only when branches rub or to emphasize a handsome branch or trunk. Included here are the Higan cherry (*P. subhirtella*), the Japanese flowering cherry (*P. serrulata*), also the Japanese flowering apricot, *P. Mume,* as well as the table apricots.

GARDEN PLUM — SUMMER–WINTER

Prune these trees to a modified leader (as for sweet and sour cherries) while young; very little pruning is required after the scaffold is developed until they begin to bear. Then in summer cut out long, whippy shoots, thin the crown to let in light and preserve the fruit spurs inside the tree, and head-back vigorous growers rather severely. A little pruning each year at the crown will keep a crop of vigorous shoots coming on; trees left unpruned are soon full of stubby branches with poor spurs. Included here are the common plum (*P. domestica* and varieties), also the Damson and Bullace (*P. institia*), Mirabelle (*P. institia syriaca*), Green-gage, and 'Reine Claude' (*P. institia italica*).

FLOWERING PLUM — SPRING–SUMMER

Grow these as bushy, little trees with short trunks or as shrubs. They produce more or less upright branches that need little pruning but you may drop-prune (Chapter 2) them to thin out the inner wood. In areas where borers are a problem, start with the bush-form. These vigorous garden ornamentals may be cut freely for the house; some may be forced in early spring. Cut them back about a third when you plant. Included here are the cherry plum (*P. cerasifera*), the purple-leaf plum (*P. c. atropurpurea*), which is the purple-leaf cherry plum of the nurseries, the purple-leaf hybrid (*P. Blireana*); also the flowering plum (*P. triloba*).

ALMOND — WINTER

When you plant them, prune one- or two-year-old grafted trees severely. Select a strong leader and three or four well-spaced side branches with wide crotches. Cut away all other wood. Cut back any shoots that develop from the side branches to at least 18 inches from the trunk. If there are no shoots, rub off the buds that will form shoots with a gloved hand. During the next three or four years, allow two or three more well-spaced side branches to develop. Then head-back the leader (*do not remove it*) to encourage crown branching. In winter, prune bearing trees by removing about half of the previous year's growth, all weak wood, and rubbing branches. Selected cultivars of almond, *P. Amygdalus,* will grow wherever apricots bear so long as you have a hot, dry place for them.

PRUNUS Laurocerasus CHERRY-LAUREL SUMMER

Cut back seedlings or rooted cuttings hard to build a dense bush. Prune according to your purpose for a loose informal shrub, a topiary specimen (Chapter 4), or shear for a hedge.

PRUNUS Persica PEACH LATE WINTER–EARLY SPRING

These are low-crowned, small trees, whether ornamental or fruiting cultivars. Prune flowering peach trees as needed to build a rather ball-shaped top on a clean trunk. A little pinching and thinning of newly set plants usually does the job.

At planting, cut whips for fruit trees to 18 to 24 inches; be sure there are several buds below your cut. If there are side branches, shorten these to a single, outward-facing bud. If your new tree comes with several well-developed branches, thin these to three or four, head them back about halfway and remove the central leader after planting. The next spring, your young tree should have a number of side branches. Select three or four strong ones that are well spaced around the tree and remove all others; head-back the scaffold branches about one-third, again cutting to an outward-facing bud. If the central leader remains, remove it at this pruning. Your tree is now an open-center specimen.

The second spring select three or four well-spaced side branches on each of the main limbs—these should fill in sideways, not up or down, though a slight inclination toward the open center is all right—and remove all other small branches. Head-back the side branches halfway or less if they appear very vigorous and whippy.

The third spring, repeat the selection of well-placed side branches on last season's extension growth of the main limbs, and make the same selection of well-spaced, strong wood on the side branches saved the previous spring. Do not remove ingrowing branches at this time if they are sturdy and fit into the framework because fruit will be borne on these next year.

Prune bearing trees in late winter or early spring; remove all weak or injured wood, thin and head-back heavily budded, year-old wood to six to ten flower buds, and remove some ingrowing shoots to preserve an open center.

You can grow peaches north of their normal range by training them flat on a south wall. String wires several inches away from the wall to make a supporting grid. Fan out the branches but don't try for a geometric design because peach trees won't cooperate. The pruning technique is the same as above, but in only two planes. Dwarf trees, both flowering and fruiting, tend to be too leafy. This is no problem for the ornamentals, but for good fruit, you have to thin the tree, cutting out enough inside leafy twigs to let light and air penetrate to the center.

PRUNUS serrula WINTER

Prune this small ornamental tree to feature bark on trunk and main limbs. A good way is to maintain a clean whip for 6 to 8 feet, then allow five or six widely spaced limbs to develop. Keep these free of branches for 2 feet or more from the trunk and drop-prune (Chapter 2) the crown of young trees severely to get heavy, relatively unbranched limbs.

PSEUDOTSUGA Douglasii DOUGLAS-FIR LATE SPRING

Shear the new growth on seedlings to develop a dense conical plant. From knee-high on, cut back new growth on branch ends to half or less, and new side growth even more. Older trees should not be pruned.

PTELEA trifoliata WAFER-ASH, HOP-TREE SUMMER

Grow this native as a large, loose shrub or a small tree with a stubby trunk. On young plants, to tighten growth, cut long shoots back halfway or more and reduce all new growth about a third. For a tree, strip all side branches from a whip; side buds will break repeatedly so that you will probably not get more than a few feet of clean trunk. As branches develop, strip them off for several feet up the trunk; then cut them back to an inside bud so the tree will be narrow.

PUNICA Granatum nana DWARF POMEGRANATE SPRING
Grow as hedge plants or individual specimens in any frost-free garden. These may be short-lived unless pruned regularly. Shear a hedge if it looks to rough, but don't keep it so smooth you lose the handsome orange flowers. Prune inner twiggy branches out of older specimens and clip over the new growth to keep the plant compact. These shrubs can be pruned into various forms or trimmed as gnarled, miniature treelike specimens. With flowering garden shrubs, remove about a fourth of the oldest wood at the basal crown each spring, and clip back new shoots that grow enough beyond the general spread of the plant to make it look unkempt.

Purple-wreath see **PETREA**

PYRACANTHA FIRETHORN SUMMER–LATE WINTER
Prune these hard when young to develop a tight bush; prune older specimens heavily to restrict growth. Cut back new growth as you wish; flowers are produced from older wood. This shrub shows to best advantage trained and trimmed into patterns on a wall or around a post. Always cut at a crotch since stubs die back, causing rot in a branch. Don't let old, bush-form plants become too dense or apple scab and fireblight may become serious problems. While most pruning is done in summer, renovate old bushes with the loppers in late winter, cutting out the oldest trunks to the ground.

PYRUS PEAR WINTER
Prune young trees of table kinds lightly; remove weak or crowded branches and head-back overlong shoots. Prune to a shape that fits growth habit, through a modified leader, as with apples, is a fair compromise for most kinds. Prune older trees severely to encourage fruiting; cut back year-old wood to half or less and remove about half of last year's shoots to let light and air into the crown. If fireblight shows up, prune severely, cutting well below diseased shoots as soon as the wilt is apparent. Dip pruner in a disinfectant between cuts.

Prune espalier-trained pears like apple trees. European growers favor cordons and pyramids for select table cultivars. Cordon training is similar to espalier training but the specimens are free standing.

(see Chapter 4). For a pyramid-trained tree allow carefully spaced branches to develop from the trunk, usually about 6 inches apart, all round the tree. Cut back side branches severely to keep them short, almost unbranched, and heavy. When a cone-shaped specimen has been built up, crowning at 8 to 10 feet, let fruit branches develop sparingly at the branch ends to clothe the pyramid. Cut back each branch to two or three spurs. These trees have no inside foliage and produce exhibition quality fruit that is beautifully colored since it gets a maximum of sunlight.

Let the ornamental Callery pear, *P. Calleryana,* and the willow-leaved *P. salicifolia* take their natural habit, but thin out the inside wood and cut back too vigorous shoots. For good appearance, thin the drooping branches of the weeping form of the willow-leaved type.

Queen's creeper see **PETREA**

QUERCUS OAK SUMMER–WINTER

Prune saplings to a strong leader by shortening side branches by about a third as they are produced. You may cut off lower branches as a young tree grows taller, leaving a clean trunk for as much as a third of the total height. White oaks tend to develop V-crotches fairly early due to double leaders; always remove one branch to maintain a true leader. Some black oaks, notably the pin, *Q. palustris,* and its near relatives, are pyramidal when young; from about twenty years on, the lower branches turn down. Some years later when the pyramidal habit is lost and the crown opens out, these lower limbs die and fall. For headroom, you may prune up lawn trees of this group by removing limbs at the trunk without endangering the final form of the tree, but do not cut back the end of a vigorously growing oak branch. Instead remove the branch at a crotch or at the trunk; ugly sprouts appear if the branch is stubbed off. Mature oak trees need only maintenance pruning, and a minimum is best.

Raspberry see **RUBUS**
Rat-stripper see **PACHISTIMA**
Redbud see **CERCIS**
Red-cedar see **JUNIPERUS**
Redwood see **SEQUOIA**

RHAMNUS BUCKTHORN SPRING–SUMMER

Tree-forms need no special pruning. You may head-back overgrown shrub forms by drop-pruning (Chapter 2); seldom, if ever, remove old canes at the base of a shrub. Cut back tops of hedges just before new growth occurs and shear once or twice through the summer if they look ragged.

RHODODENDRON LATE SPRING–LATE WINTER

Pinch tender new shoots to two or three leaves to induce branching and nip out spent blossom heads at the same time in late spring. If you prune after midsummer, you will probably lose next year's flowers. Research indicates that renovation of very old plants requires one or two years of heavy mulching, feeding, and watering before you use the lopper; when a plant has had a chance to build up a vigorous root system with this treatment, in late winter, cut back one or two old trunks to 6-inch stubs. These should sprout new growth in spring; then the next winter, you can cut back more old branches. Save only two or three sturdy shoots on each stump; cut off weaker, crowded ones.

RHODOTYPOS JETBEAD EARLY SUMMER

When bushes get dense with dead twigs, cut back some of the oldest canes to the ground. Then pinch out basal shoots to encourage low branching. These shrubs tend to be bare-legged; manuring will stimulate new growth to help fill them out. Don't clip back the top, as many folks do, for plants will not fill out below but will grow bunchy at the ends of bare sticks.

RHUS SUMAC WINTER

The fine-twigged sorts, like *R. aromatica,* the fragrant sumac, need almost no pruning; just remove at the base, branches that spread too wide, and if desirable, restrict height by drop-pruning (Chapter 2). Except for removal of crowded branches, leave unpruned the heavy-caned types like the staghorn sumac, *R. typhina.* Cut out root sprouts with a sharp spade.

RIBES CURRANT WINTER

When you set them out, cut back young plants halfway. Try to buy plants that can be trimmed to three wide-spread stems. *Never* head-back canes on established bushes. Reduce the length of side branches, and cut out crowded and weak ones. Cut to the ground weak and old twiggy canes. *Fruit is borne at the base of year-old wood and on short lateral spurs of older wood. Let no canes remain longer than three years.* Your goal is an open plant with about evenly divided numbers of one, two, and three-year-old canes. Trim back laterals on these canes to two or three buds. Watch for borers in the canes; cut out infested ones at the crown and keep a covering of DDT on all canes through the next spring and summer. Some varieties produce canes close to the ground; cut these off before they bend over and root.

ROBINIA LOCUST, FALSE-ACACIA, OR ROSE-ACACIA SUMMER–WINTER

To insure a clean leader, prune saplings of shade-tree kinds rather severely. Head back halfway the whippy branches on young trees to develop a compact crown. Avoid digging into roots of older specimens as they sucker freely, especially after roots have been disturbed. Every year while it is young, cut back severely the false-locust, *R. PseudoAcacia Rehderi.* This will develop a globe-shaped head. Leave older trees unpruned or shear them in summer. Rose-acacia, *R. hispida,* suckers freely; avoid pruning healthy canes, and wear heavy gloves to pull out suckers in wet weather. Ask your nurseryman for *R. hispida macrophylla* with no spines, much better flowers, and no suckers. It is grafted on the Shipmast strain of black locust, therefore no suckers. All cane-type false-acacias are best grown in a thicket; grub out crowded and spent canes as necessary (illus., p. 156).

Rock-rose see **CISTUS**
Rock-spirea see **HOLODISCUS**

ROSA ROSE EARLY SPRING–SUMMER–FALL

Before setting out new bushes, prune both tops and roots; cut back injured roots to points where they are sound and undamaged; cut out injured canes entirely. Try to equalize the amount of cut-back tops and trimmed roots.

Prune plants for bloom; for the most part, modern breeding aims at flowers rather than ornamental bushes. Study the illustrations that show a bush in various stages of pruning. Early in spring, when danger

SHADE-TREE PATTERNS. Most shade trees grow with a tall straight trunk or with a short trunk and a spreading cluster of upright branches rising from it. This fine, old black locust, *Robinia,* with the characteristic straight trunk has been pruned to bring out the interesting contortions of the main limbs. The horse chestnut behind it with a short trunk has developed several wide crotches and strong upright branches in the manner of the American elm. Before pruning a young shade tree, try to see a mature specimen of the same kind so you will be familiar with the growth form. Then prune to control and enhance the natural beauty of your tree. *Author photo*

of a heavy freeze is past, cut back established Hybrid Teas, Grandifloras, Floribundas, Polyanthas, and other bedding roses to sound, green wood. Remove weak, crowded, awkward, and winter-injured canes at the base, also any with discolored bark. If you save three or four evenly distributed, thumb-sized canes, you will have roses galore. The idea is to prune for an open center so that sun and air reach all parts of the bush.

Your wiry Floribundas and Polyanthas may be twiggy and difficult to get into, but for best results try to clear up the centers and trim back the tips. Trim miniature bushes the same as the standard types, but you may want to use a manicure scissors. The rather tender Noisettes are pruned scarcely at all. Just cut out weak wood and shoots that tend to overgrow desirable branches.

Because rose canes are soft and pithy and bruise easily, be sure to use a clean well-adjusted, *sharp* scissors-action pruner. When you have finished your early spring pruning, spray those scratched and cut-back canes with lime-sulfur. Mix to dormant strength. Through the summer when a flower fades, remove it, except on the species roses. Cut stems carrying but one bloom back to the first leaf that bears five leaflets, but if those leaves grow toward the *inside* of the bush, drop down for your cut to the next *outward-facing* leaf. It is the bud in the axis of the leaf that will make a new flower-bearing shoot. If your plant has flowers in clusters, nip out each bloom as it fades; when the last one droops, cut back the same way as for a one-bloom stalk. Keep in mind that if you cut very long stems early in the year, you sacrifice lots of summer and fall flowers.

Prune the Large-flowered Climbers—Hybrid Tea and the once- and repeat-blooming types—very little when you set them out. If they are cut back severely they often lose their long-cane habit and grow bush-form. These climbers produce few new basal canes; *they bloom on new shoots from last year's wood.* In spring, prune sparingly, removing only weak, dead, and, at times, worn-out shoots. Shorten the side growth on older canes about two-thirds or just cut back to clean healthy growth. Keep old wood so long as it is productive. About every three or four years, you will find it necessary to remove at the ground-line one or more of the oldest dried-up canes. But keep your pruning to a minimum with careful thinning out of canes and snipping off of twiggy branches. Depending on space, remove one or two weaker new shoots, and spent flowers through summer as for bush roses.

Unlike the Large-flowered Climbers, Ramblers are cut back to 12 inches or less at planting time. They bloom on young wood made the *previous summer.* Consequently two-year-old canes are no longer very productive and should be removed. New canes usually originate from the base. In early summer, immediately after plants have bloomed, take them down from the trellis. Cut to the crown the canes that have flowered; thin out the thick crop of new canes, saving only half a dozen or so of the strongest. Retie these to the trellis. With Ramblers, you prune to produce a new plant above the ground every year.

On Rose Trees, cut the heads back hard in spring to 6 to 12 inches

LARGE-FLOWERED CLIMBING ROSES. After big, well-established plants have bloomed, remove at the base, or source, A, one or two of the very dry old canes to allow room for new canes, as B. Most of these will be produced higher up but from older canes. Cut back flowering stems to two or three leaf buds C; these will send out new side branches for bloom next year. Try to maintain a balance of new, year-old, and two-year-old canes. In spring, prune out winter-injured sections of wood. Anytime you see sucker growth at the base, D, remove it and, if possible, below the soil line. Based on drawing by Léonie Bell in *Climbing Roses* by Helen Van Pelt Wilson

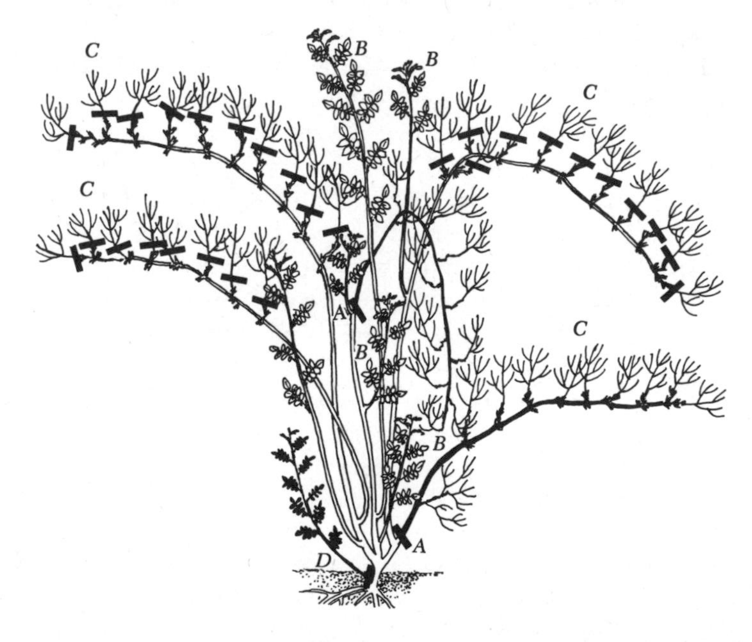

PRUNING BUSH ROSES. Figure 1 shows a bare-root rose that needs considerable pruning. Remove weak and injured canes; head-back strong canes to an outside bud at 8 to 12 inches; cut back roots to healthy, unbranched growth. When a rose blossom begins to shatter as in Figure 2, cut back the cane to a five-leaflet leaf, preferably one with a bud pointing toward the outside of the bush. For sturdier bushes and more late flowers, retain as much foliage as possible by cutting short stems for bouquets. Figure 3 shows an established garden rose, a Hybrid Tea, (it could be a Grandiflora or a Floribunda just as well), in late fall after leaves have fallen. Blooms have been cut back but the bush is twiggy and full. Figure 4 shows the same plant early the next spring after it has been cut back for another season's growth.

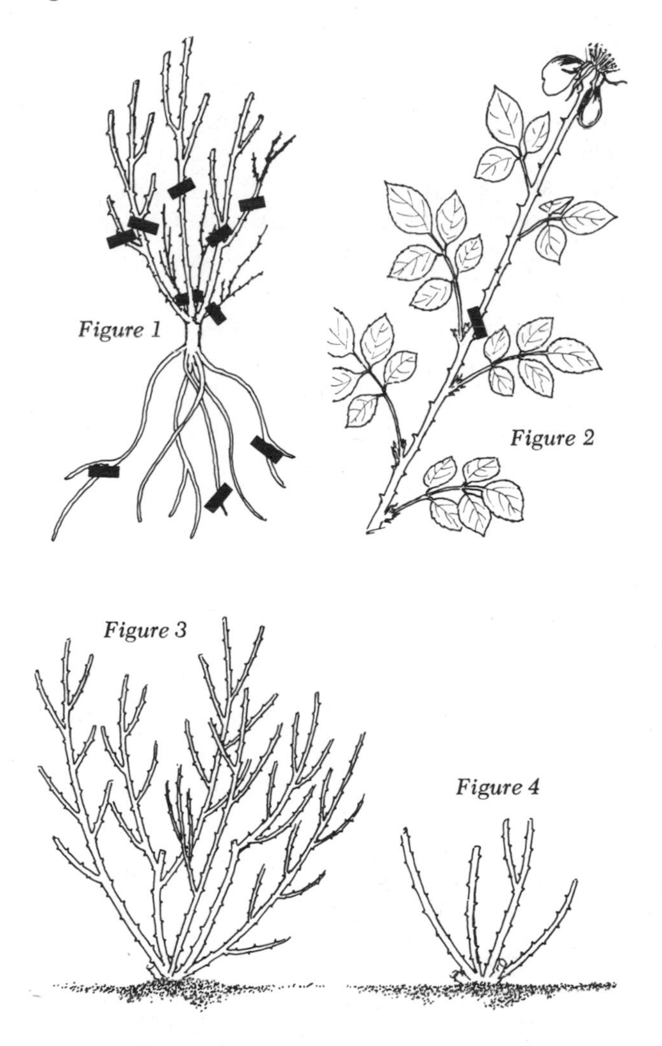

above the union. Remove all weak canes at that point and cut back others to make a symmetrical head of three or four buds for each strong cane. Where winters are severe, shorten canes in late fall to facilitate protection of the head and union. Then finish the pruning in spring.

Most Species Roses are grown in informal hedges or as ornamental specimen shrubs. They need almost no pruning except the regular removal of winter-killed wood—more in some years than others—and the cleaning up of tangled, non-blooming growth at the ground from the centers of old bushes. This is a fiercesome task requiring sharp pruners and heavy gloves. (Sometimes it is easier to cut the whole plant to the ground and let it renew itself completely.) The object in pruning species is to retain the natural symmetry of the plant—upright, broad, or drooping—while promoting flowering. Many species especially the Spinossimas and Rugosas are ruined if headed back, and all are deformed if tops are bobbed regardless of habit. Don't cut off faded flowers; by fall, these will have become handsome, colorful fruits.

Rose-acacia see **ROBINIA**
Rose-of-Sharon see **HIBISCUS**
Rowan see **SORBUS**

RUBUS BRAMBLES: BLACKBERRY, RASPBERRY, DEWBERRY EARLY SPRING–SUMMER

Canes of brambles are biennial; the first year, they grow up from the crown or as root suckers; by midsummer they send out side branches. The second spring, short blooming twigs develop on these side branches and, after the fruit has ripened, the entire cane dies. Train upright blackberries and red raspberries on individual stakes, or space them along a single taut wire fastened to posts. When ground is soft, pull out all young excess root suckers; cut back the new canes to 30 to 36 inches; branches will develop after canes are cut back. The next spring cut back the branches to about 12 inches for larger, better developed fruit. After fruiting is over, cut out the spent canes. By this time, a crop of new canes will be growing. Cut out at the crown all but three or four of the strongest and pull out the suckers.

Trailing blackberries, dewberries, and black raspberries, none of which throws suckers, may be handled the same way in the home garden but, for greater yield, string two wires to posts; spread canes from the *outside* of the clump along the *lower* wire; tie canes in the *middle* of the clump to the *upper* wire. Don't cut back new canes of dewberries and trailing black raspberries; instead thin the crowns to about twelve canes for dewberries and about six canes for trailing black raspberries. Thin out upright black raspberries to three to five canes and head them back to 36 inches. Early in spring, cut back side branches of all of these to 12 inches; in summer remove spent canes and excess shoots. Treat everbearing strains of brambles the same way, only wait to remove bearing canes until fall frosts.

Loganberries, youngberries, boysenberries, and other exotic brambles are treated similarly, but they are usually more rampant, requiring wider spacing, higher supports, and more vigorous removal of suckers. Failure to control suckers and anthracnose disease are the

PRUNING AND THINNING RASPBERRIES. Figure 1 shows a red raspberry patch after pruning and thinning. New canes are usually cut back to about knee high. Old canes are removed as they finish bearing. Here many canes have been removed so the rest can be nicely spaced. Figure 2 shows an unpruned black raspberry after the old canes have been removed but before new growth has been cut back. Figure 3 shows the bush after new growth has been thinned and cut back. This plant should now be staked.

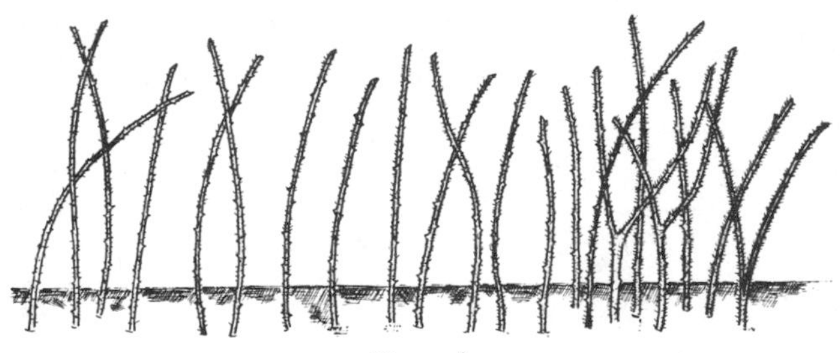

Figure 1

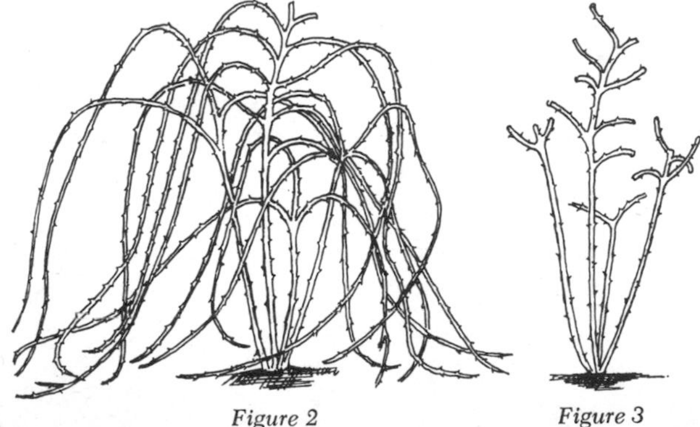

Figure 2 *Figure 3*

main causes for failure with brambles. While there are ways to utilize sucker growth for productivity, the home-gardener will be wise to remove all suckers and, right after spring pruning, to drench dormant crowns and canes with lime-sulfur solution for disease control.

Russian-olive see **ELAEAGNUS**
Sagebrush see **ARTEMISIA**
St.-John's-wort see **HYPERICUM**
Salal see **GAULTHERIA**

SALIX WILLOW WINTER

To get sturdy shoots on vigorous roots, cut back newly planted willow whips almost to the ground. Train tree-types, as weeping willow and silver willow, to a single stem until this is as thick as a broomstick; then let well-spaced side branches develop but continue to limit growth that may interfere with the leader. In winter, go through the interior of older trees and take out unsightly water sprouts and deteriorating branches. Never stub-back a willow limb or it will produce an unsightly broom of whippy shoots. Allow shrubby sorts, like pussy-willow and arctic willow, to develop naturally, but thin out crowded interior branches. As the shrubs become too bulky for space or wood begins to deteriorate, cut them to the ground; they will renew themselves in two to three years. To replace willow trees in soggy ground, saw off upright 2½- to 4-inch diameter limbs from healthy trees. In late winter, dig post holes about 2 feet deep where each new tree is to stand. Set the limbs in the holes, ram the soil tight around them, and stake. Thin tops to three or four branches. Most of the planted limbs will strike root and grow well by the next spring.

SAMBUCUS ELDERBERRY LATE WINTER

Prune tree-forms only enough to preserve a well-shaped, symmetrical head that is fairly open. A little cutting out of in-growing branches to a crotch every two or three years does it. Common green shrub-forms may be left almost unpruned; just remove a few of the oldest shoots at the ground from time to time, and use a sharp spade to cut out suckers that come up away from the base. When a shrub looks ragged, cut it back hard to force out a new crop of canes from the crown. But every year cut back golden-leaved and variegated forms, leaving short, heavy trunks that bear knobs of well-budded cane stubs. These will produce the vigorous new shoots that are the most colorful.

SANTOLINA LAVENDER-COTTON SPRING–SUMMER

Go over these in early spring and nip out winter-injured shoots. Cut plants back hard after flowers fade. If there is no bloom, shear or cut back in mid-August. Avoid pruning after Labor Day because new growth produced at the end of the season will be winter killed.

SARCOCOCCA SWEET-BOX SPRING

Cut back old canes to the ground as they show signs of deteriorating. Root-prune whole clumps with a spade when they spread too far; you can use the severed canes to extend your planting. Avoid cutting back canes halfway for subsequent branching will be dog-legged and unattractive.

Sarvisberry see **AMELANCHIER**

SASSAFRAS LATE WINTER

Let young trees go unpruned; they will branch low and form a perfect head without your interference. You may raise the height of older trees by sawing off low branches. Avoid digging into the roots as they sprout much too freely when injured; pull out young root sprouts in spring when the ground is soft. This tree may be trained and pruned into gnarled, windswept forms for the rock garden or grown as bonsai in a container. Remove branches and pinch new growth severely if you want to limit development.

SATUREJA montana WINTER SAVORY EARLY SPRING–SUMMER

Pinch young plants severely to make them branch. As new growth reaches 3 to 4 inches, shear it off to dry for kitchen use. Early in spring, cut back all plants hard. Since these deteriorate in three to five years even when pruned tight, keep a fresh supply of rooted heel cuttings coming along.

SCIADOPITYS verticillata UMBRELLA- OR PARASOL-PINE SUMMER

Prune as needed to remove rival leaders. To thicken the tree and limit size, cut back new growth halfway. Shear plants used in hedges. Where space is no problem, let this plant go its way, but it takes kindly to tight shearing and container culture.

SEQUOIA REDWOOD, BIG-TREE SUMMER

Prune seedlings and young trees to a single leader; you may judiciously clip back new growth but take care to preserve the rippling contours of the natural habit. Trees are best left untrimmed once a dense body with a single leader has developed.

Service-tree see **SORBUS**
Shadblow see **AMELANCHIER**
Sheepkill see **KALMIA**

SHEPHERDIA BUFFALO-BERRY EARLY SPRING

Prune this shrub as little as possible to avoid ugly scars and kinks in the trunks. In the South, cut out blighted wood each year. In the North, it does not blight but grows very well. In general, remove the oldest trunks and awkward, unbranched shoots from old specimens; pinch basal shoots to induce low branching.

Silk-oak see **GREVILLEA robusta**
Silktree see **ALBIZZIA**
Silverbell-tree see **HALESIA**
Silver-berry see **ELAEAGNUS**
Silver-vine see **ACTINIDIA**

SKIMMIA SUMMER

These rather tender, small, broad-leaved evergreen shrubs need little pruning; remove weak, hard, older branches from established plants, and pinch back new shoots to keep growth shapely.

Smoke-tree see **COTINUS**
Snowball see **HYDRANGEA**
Snowberry see **SYMPHORICARPOS**
Snow-in-summer see **MELALEUCA linariifolia**

SOPHORA JAPANESE PAGODA-TREE or CHINESE SCHOLAR-TREE MIDSUMMER–FALL

With shade trees, trim whips and saplings to a dominant leader; for two years, strip off all side branches in the fall; then head-back laterals until the trunk is wrist thick. I prefer to grow these lacy trees with multiple stems, thinning inner branches and shortening overlong side branches by cutting back to a crotch. Thin the weeping type to make the most of the handsome, writhing growth of limbs and trunk. If your old specimen becomes twiggy and dense, drop-prune (Chapter 2) the top to relieve the crowded condition; two summers later, drop-prune it again, removing many small terminal branches at a crotch.

SORBARIA FALSE-SPIREA EARLY SPRING–SUMMER

As flowers fade in summer, or wait until early the next spring, reduce the new flower-bearing shoots on large shrubs to three or four leaves. For a dramatic effect, cut canes to the ground each spring, forcing new growth. These sucker freely so keep a sharp spade handy to dig out unwanted sprouts.

SORBUS MOUNTAIN-ASH, WHITEBEAM, ROWAN, SERVICE-TREE WINTER

Keep large shade trees, as the service-tree, S. *domestica,* and the whitebeam, S. *Aria,* to a single leader until they are 12 to 15 feet high; at the same time, lightly cut back side branches each year and remove some at the trunk, saving the best-spaced, wide-crotched ones. Raise older trees by removing lower branches as needed. Grow the ornamental berried kinds like mountain-ash informally as single specimens or with multiple trunks. Thin out enough to show the trunk and head-back side branches by drop-pruning (Chapter 2). Columnar variants scarcely need pruning but you may shear them while young to build up a tight well-formed scaffold.

Sorrel-tree see **OXYDENDRUM arboreum**
Sour cherry see **PRUNUS**
Sour gum see **NYSSA**
Sourwood see **OXYDENDRUM arboreum**
Southernwood see **ARTEMISIA**
Spice-bush see **LINDERA**
Spindle-tree see **EUONYMUS**

SPIREA BRIDAL-WREATH, HARDHACK SPRING

Prune spring-bloomers as flowers fade. Those with ARCHING branches and a tight clump of canes like S. *Vanhouttei* need only a little thinning; every year, cut out a few of the crowded old canes at the ground. Don't cut back tops or these forms will lose their grace and get broomy. UPRIGHT spring bloomers, like bridal-wreath, S. *prunifolia,* also need little pruning; occasionally remove old canes with many dead twigs. Use a sharp spade to cut back clumps as most of these sucker freely. SUMMER-FLOWERING KINDS, as S. *Billiardii,* S. *japonica,* S. *Bumalda,* and 'Anthony Waterer', are in this group, and may be pruned heavily in early spring. Since bloom is produced on new wood, cut back canes to two or three buds. Or lightly prune early in spring for more bush and perhaps smaller but more abundant flowers. When in doubt, *don't* prune is a good rule-of-thumb for spireas. With the newer tiny spireas, as S. *japonica alpina* and S. *nipponica* 'Snowbound', help to preserve their small stature by pinching out vigorous, upright shoots; and every three or four years go through the plants to nip out dead and twiggy shoots.

Spruce see **PICEA**
Spurge-laurel see **DAPHNE**

STAPHYLEA BLADDER-NUT SPRING–SUMMER

To develop bushy specimens, pinch new growth on young plants; older plants require little pruning but pinch new shoots, especially those near the base of the plant, to induce branching. Some species, like S. *trifolia,* spreading from underground runners, form large thickets; restrict these by spading out suckers that appear beyond the desired limit of the shrub. The American bladder-nut, S. *trifolia,* may be kept to 10 feet or less; others, particularly the Caucasian S. *colchica* and European S. *pinnata* must be allowed to reach 12 feet or more. You can grow the Chinese S. *holocarpa* as a small tree by pruning it to a single leader and removing all basal shoots and low side branches.

STEPHANANDRA LATE SPRING

Use judgment with these; their garden value lies in their graceful arching form. Cut out enough of the oldest canes to the ground to keep the bush from being a tangled mass. Don't pinch or cut back branches as the plant then becomes broomy. If this is used in informal hedges, thin out old wood, cutting it to the ground every year but don't clip back or shear the top.

STEPHANOTIS MADAGASCAR-JASMINE EARLY SPRING

Cut back sturdy stems as necessary to keep this plant within bounds on its trellis in the greenhouse or outdoors in the South. Remove weak and dangling branches completely. Tie new growth to the supports to keep the vine open. Old, tangled plants may be fed heavily, then cut to the ground; thin out the new shoots to three or four. Pot-grown specimens require additional pruning through the summer to keep them manageable, but late pruning cuts away flowering wood. Old, container-grown specimens become hard and bloom poorly, so it's a good idea to keep a few rooted cuttings on hand to replace the woody plants that must be discarded.

STEWARTIA LATE WINTER

Grow these as large shrubs or small low-branching trees; you need only thin out crowded inside branches and cut back too vigorous shoots from the previous year. Plants assume a good shape with little assistance.

Strawberry-bush see **EUONYMUS**
Strawberry-tree see **ARBUTUS**

STREPTOSOLEN Jamesonii

This frost-sensitive evergreen shrub blooms best on vigorous new wood. Cut it back hard as it goes out of bloom, removing almost to the base all wood older than three years, and reducing the rest to fit the situation. Old trunks cut to 8-inch stubs soon throw a crop of sucker-like shoots that bear great panicles of flowers. The natural habit of a shrub pruned to new wood is arching, and the graceful form is lost if you tie up the stems in a tight sheaf. Old shrubs that have ceased flowering may be brought back to production by reducing all canes to short stubs; thin out each stub to three or four new shoots until the plant regains its vigor.

Sugarberry see **CELTIS**
Sumac see **RHUS**
Summer-lilac see **BUDDLEIA**
Sweetbay see **MAGNOLIA**
Sweet-box see **SARCOCOCCA**
Sweet cherry see **PRUNUS**
Sweet-gale see **MYRICA**
Sweet-gum-tree see **LIQUIDAMBAR Styraciflua**
Sweetleaf see **SYMPLOCOS**

Sweet-pepperbush see **CLETHRA**
Sweetshade see **HYMENOSPORUM flavum**
Sweet-shrub see **CALYCANTHUS**
Sycamore see **PLATANUS**

SYMPHORICARPOS SNOWBERRY, WAXBERRY, BUCK-BRUSH EARLY SPRING

Cut out old twiggy canes but save all well-spaced, slender, arching ones without cutting back. These rather diffuse, nondescript shrubs invite pruning but cutting back tops produces witches' brooms. Some kinds, particularly the native Indian-currant or buck-brush, S. *orbiculatus,* spread far by runners that lie on or just under the ground. Cut these off close to the parent plant and then pull them up; sprouting shrubs along runners will come out with them.

SYMPLOCOS SWEETLEAF SUMMER

Every four or five years remove a few of the oldest trunks and head back strong, unbranched shoots to three or four joints the summer they appear. You may grow seedlings from these into small, refined trees; clip off side branches the year after they are produced and immediately remove any near-terminal shoots that threaten to interfere with the leader. When you have a clean 4- to 5-foot stem, let the plant develop naturally, only removing basal shoots that break from the trunk or below ground.

SYRINGA LILAC SPRING–SUMMER

Except to remove shoots that break from below the graft (the knobby place on the stem), do not prune a young lilac at all for four or five years. Then after it blooms, remove one or two of the oldest canes each year or so at the ground line, and thin out basal shoots to three or four well-spaced canes. When old bushes grow to 8 feet or more with dry, brittle wood and flowers only at the top, prune hard to renew the bushes. First, cut out enough basal shoots so you can reach inside the plant. Then you can be drastic and cut down all but half a dozen of the *young* flowering canes and *all* the old, rough, bark-covered wood to the ground. If you have the nerve to do this in early summer after bloom is past, your bushes won't look like much. However, new growth will reach above 3 feet by fall and plants will look respectable the next spring when canes will be so tall you will want to cut them back to 5 or 6 feet. The second spring you will probably have bloom again.

Or, you can remove some of the oldest canes each year over a period of two or three years, thus keeping up a supply of flowers while reconditioning your bush. In any case, get rid at once of any trunks that have scaly bark and are gnarled from borers. Finally, head-back at a crotch any disproportionately tall canes that remain.

For good looks, snip off spent lilac blooms before seed-heads form, although plants will continue to flower without this grooming. Cut back to the first leaves below the flower. Through the summer, watch trunks and crown for sawdust, evidence of borers. Remove any infested canes and burn them; then apply a systemic insecticide to the root area.

If you grow the Japanese lilac, S. *amurensis japonica,* as a gnarled, single or multiple-trunk tree, rub off side buds in spring, allowing only a few branches to develop below the terminal. Shorten these to three or four leaves. At about 4 feet, let the plant develop almost naturally, removing some branches as they reach thumb-thickness.

REMOVING SEED PODS FROM LILACS. For best bloom, take off spent flowers at A, the base of the bloom stalk. Where tender new shoots show a single terminal bud, as at B, cut back a little to a node or two below the tip of the shoot. This encourages branching. Always leave any shoots with two terminal buds, as at C, since these are probably flower buds.

This leaves a crooked trunk with just a few side branches, a "character" plant in ten years or less.

With standard lilacs, trim the heads close. Remove spent blooms immediately, and pinch new growth at four or five leaves. In early spring, shorten it to two joints if it does not show flower buds.

Tamarisk see **TAMARIX**

TAMARIX TAMARISK EARLY SPRING–SUMMER

These plants may be set close, cut back hard, and developed into a sheared hedge or grown as specimens and pruned according to type. *T. anglica, T. parviflora,* and *T. tetandra* develop into large shrubs; every third or fourth summer prune out a little of the oldest wood at the base; also head-back new growth after flowering but clip carefully to avoid a sheared look. With *T. odessana, T. pentandra,* and their garden forms, cut canes back hard, to two or three buds near the base of last year's wood. For best results, develop a clump of four to eight 6-inch trunks, each bearing a cluster of short spurs to furnish the new shoots; cut back to the spurs each year. If you don't know which tamarisk you have, just grow it as a natural, unpruned shrub for two or three years. If it does not flower satisfactorily, cut it back to 6-inch stubs. These will produce new growth. Early the next spring, cut this back to two or three buds. New growth from these buds should flower in midsummer.

Tara-vine see **ACTINIDIA**

TAXODIUM BALD-CYPRESS, POND-CYPRESS SPRING

Train seedlings and young trees to a single trunk; cut off secondary leaders where they originate on the trunk. You may shear young plants for three or four years to make them fill out, but don't prune older trees. And don't cut your tree down when it turns brown and sheds its "greenery" in fall. This is a needle tree that loses leaves and branchlets in autumn, and greens up again next year.

TAXUS YEW EARLY SPRING–SUMMER

Shear hedges and topiary specimens hard in early spring and as needed through summer. Protect the leader of young upright yews by removing secondary leaders as they appear. Trim young spreading and vase-shaped kinds as inverted cones for three or four years to make them develop a full center. Prune older yews as they appear to need it, removing new growth or cutting it back after it has hardened to the size you want. If a spreading yew gets too thick and looks "stuffed" from repeated heading back, reach in with loppers and cut out a few finger-sized old branches way down in the plant. Contrary to most recommendations, my yews get a substantial trimming about the twentieth of December so the beautiful greenery is fresh for Christmas. If space is no problem, let your yews go untrimmed after they are about ten years old; with age, they make huge, handsome specimens. Burn yew clippings immediately as the foliage of most kinds is *poisonous* to animals and children.

THUJA ARBORVITAE SPRING–SUMMER–FALL

Most important in pruning these is not to cut beyond green leaves. You can cut way back on the rather rubbery brown branches as long as there is even a wisp of greenery—those little scaly green shoots—but if you go farther, your plant will have a bare spot forever after. Shear hedges hard in mid-spring, and once or twice through the summer. Ideally, specimen shrubs and trees should have a single trunk and you should remove competing secondary leaders as they appear, but in practice, most plants bought from the nursery are a swatch of about equal-sized leaders that can never be sorted out. Leave these unpruned, or clip back the new growth to half or more as it hardens off, but follow the natural contours of the plant to avoid a sheared look. To protect against heavy snow, late in fall reach in about two feet below the top of your tree and tie the leaders loosely together with wide strips of cloth. Then snow cannot spring the branches apart. These strips may remain for they don't show, but replace them every second or third fall to be sure they are strong enough to hold the branches.

Thunderwood see **BUMELIA**

TILIA BASSWOOD, LINDEN, LIME SUMMER OR WINTER

Train young whips to a single leader by cutting back new side branches halfway. As a sapling grows, remove limbs (for shade trees), keeping the trunk stripped for the lower third. Older lindens need little pruning, but remove any weak-crotched branches and thin the tops by drop-pruning (Chapter 2). Except the American basswood, *T. americana*, most lindens look best with all the lower branches intact and sweeping the ground but such growth is only suited to large lawns.

TIPUANA Tipu TIPU-TREE MIDWINTER

The natural habit of this frost-sensitive flowering tree is broad and flat topped, but it can be pruned several ways. Remove side branches from a sapling until it is over head-high. Then either thin the crown branches as they spread out to achieve a parasol pattern or, after the branches have made some growth, cut them back and clip the new growth for a season or two so the tree is dense and rather upright. In southern California the tipu-tree is sometimes pruned to an artificial form with tufts of foliage on evenly spaced branches, but it seems a shame to distort a tree that has such a beautiful, natural form.

Tipu-tree see **TIPUANA Tipu**
Tomato see **LYCOPERSICUM**
Tree-of-heaven see **AILANTHUS**
Trumpet-creeper see **CAMPSIS**
Trumpet-vine see **BIGNONIA**

TSUGA HEMLOCK EARLY SPRING–SUMMER

Inspect your small new hemlock to be sure it has just one leader; if you find secondary leaders, cut them out at the points of origin. The plant may look very sparse for a year or two, but in four or five years it will develop into a much better tree. Older trees need no pruning. Shear hemlock hedges before growth resumes in spring; keep them narrow at the top and broad at the base; then the lower branches will hold their needles. A second shearing in midsummer may be necessary for a formal effect.

Tulip-poplar see **LIRIODENDRON tulipifera**
Tulip-tree see **LIRIODENDRON tulipifera**
Tupelo see **NYSSA**

ULMUS ELM MIDSUMMER

Prune young trees to straight leaders. When the American elm reaches 12 to 15 feet, let it grow naturally forming its own lovely vase shape.

In fact, most elms need little trimming save the cutting back of extra-long side branches but some hybrids and the weedier Oriental types, as the Siberian *U. pumila* and Chinese *U. parvifolia,* tend to produce twin leaders during the sapling stage. Cut off one of these leaders at the crotch as soon as it is produced. Older American elms need little maintenance pruning, but drop-prune (Chapter 2) them every ten years or so to keep branches from splitting. Heavily drop-prune the two Oriental ones every second or third year, removing as much as a third of the top each time. Contrary to custom, elms should not be "topped." The weeping elm may be kept to a formal umbrella; cut off any upright shoots; or let the tree develop naturally into a rather open, exotic specimen. For a hedge, plant year-old whips a foot apart and cut them to 2-inch stubs. Shear back new growth halfway every time it reaches 6 inches; build up a dense twiggy shape that slopes in sharply toward the top. Keep all elms free of weak, injured, or dead branches as such wood is a breeding place for the European elm-bark beetle which transmits Dutch elm disease.

Umbrella-pine see **SCIADOPITYS verticillata**

VACCINIUM BLUEBERRY, CRANBERRY, HUCKLEBERRY, WHORTLEBERRY EARLY SPRING

Native kinds used as ornamentals scarcely need pruning; occasionally take out an old cane or two at the ground so new shoots will continue to come up from the base. Tall kinds throw few shoots but some low ones spread broadly and may be cut back as required. I can't imagine anyone growing cranberries in a backyard bog but, if you do and if they grow too luxuriantly, in early spring drain the water, sand down the plants, and mow them to about 6 inches.

Wait to prune table-variety blueberries until they are three to four years old. Then remove all but one or two basal sprouts that must be saved to eventually replace very old wood. Thin out older canes to six to eight per plant, and cut out crowding twiggy wood on these. If your bushes bear generous crops of undersized berries, cut back the fruiting shoots to three to five buds. In early spring, you can identify the fruiting buds as the round fat ones, while leaf buds are more slender and pointed. After ten years, cut out one or two of the oldest canes and allow two or three more shoots to develop from the base. Some horticultural varieties of blueberries, left unpruned, grow

PRUNING CULTIVATED BLUEBERRIES. An old, unkempt bush, as Figure 1, bears small, hard fruit. Thin it out, as in Figure 2 by cutting out old, gnarled canes and twiggy branches. This will encourage the development of strong, new, basal shoots. These are then lightly pruned, as in Figure 3, to build up a globe of well-spaced, berry-bearing wood.

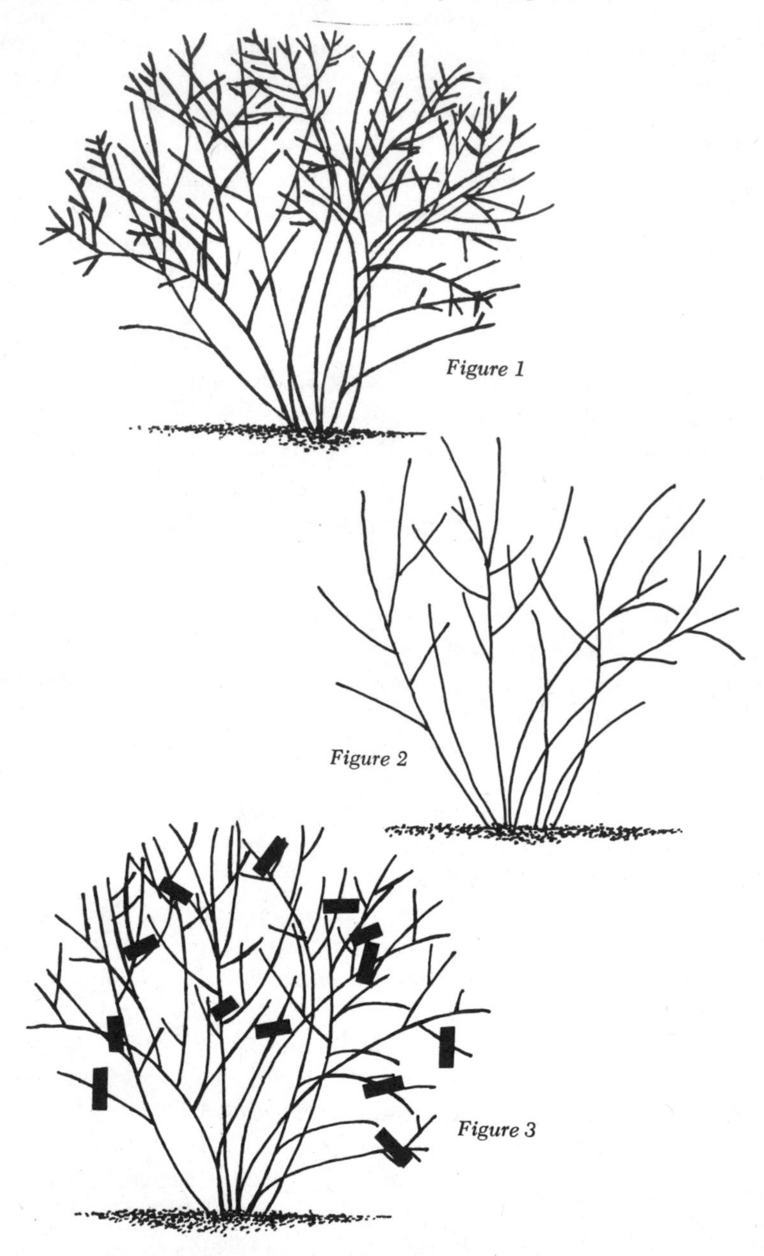

Figure 1

Figure 2

Figure 3

to 6 feet or so but the berries are small and hard. Restrict old bushes to waist high or less, and prune to keep them open and free from an excess of basal shoots.

Veronica see **HEBE**

VIBURNUM GUELDER-ROSE, BLACKHAW, NANNYBERRY, WAYFARING-TREE, CRANBERRY-BUSH — SPRING–MIDSUMMER

When you plant young bushes of this large and varied group, cut to the base some of the old, twiggy canes, leaving the vigorous young

YOUNG VIBURNUM IN NEED OF PRUNING. Two summers after planting, this twiggy little bush has made too much random new growth. *Philpott photo*

PRUNED VIBURNUM. Old wood in the center of the bush in the previous picture has been removed and piled in front of the plant; basal shoots are seen breaking just above the ground-line. If these are pinched out, they will branch and fill in around the long, leggy stems that were not pinched before as they developed. *Philpott photo*

shoots. Cut back a few of these to various heights. After this first pruning, watch for crowded branches, crossing limbs, and deteriorating wood that needs to be removed. Don't try to "shape" or limit these large shrubs—*V. tomentosum* goes to 10 feet—since none takes to heavy pruning except the dwarf or semi-dwarf cranberry bush. These may be globed formally or used for low hedges; prune them in early spring. Some of the larger types may be trained as small trees; begin with a whip; then cut back all side branches to force a straight leader. You can get several feet of clean trunk before the plant insists on branching. With standards of *V. carlcephalum* and *V. Carlesii*, early in the year, pinch out new sterile shoots to one or two joints, and later cut back spent flower stalks well into the head. Many of the newer horticultural forms are grafted on native seedlings and these rootstocks may throw shoots that can eventually dominate the more desirable crown. Watch your choice viburnum for a shoot with foreign-looking leaves; if such appears, cut it out at the point of origin, and watch for more of the same.

Virginia-creeper see **PARTHENOCISSUS**
Virgin's-bower see **CLEMATIS**

VITEX CHASTE-TREE, HEMP-TREE EARLY SPRING

In the North, prune the same as *Buddleia;* reduce all of last year's shoots to stubs with two or three buds. As these break, thin out inside shoots and pull out weak ones. Where the top is hardy, you can prune this way or just thin heavily every spring, removing about a third of the oldest wood to the ground; at the same time, head-back unbranched shoots halfway but leave branched shoots alone at full

FLOWERING SHRUB BEFORE PRUNING. Here a thickened vitex shows the effects of bad pruning with stubbed-off branches and loss of form. *Philpott photo*

FLOWERING SHRUB AFTER PRUNING. Now old wood has been removed from the bush in the previous picture and weak shoots and most side branches growing toward the center cut away at the crown. *Philpott photo*

height. As this blooms on this year's wood, heavy pruning yields a better crop of flowers. In the South, a 10-foot or greater height is usual.

VITIS GRAPE LATE WINTER

The purpose of pruning is to produce fine clusters of grapes; even vines grown on pergolas and wall trellises can be pruned for choice fruit. Cultivars of the native *V. Labrusca* or fox grape are grown over most of the United States. Selections and hybrids of the native muscadine, *V. rotundifolia,* are grown in the Southeast. The wine industry of the Pacific slope and New York State use the old-world wine grape, *V. vinifera.* The three groups are pruned differently.

In the northern and eastern states, grow Labrusca varieties—'Concord', 'Catawba', 'Moore Early', and 'Niagara' for juice, jelly, and homemade wine. The Kniffin four-arm system is commonly used for training these, but the Upright system is as good though it requires more summer manipulation. For commercial production, both systems employ two or three taut wires, but on walls and pergolas you may use latticework instead. With either system, it takes four years to produce a fruitful, well-trained vine.

Select a year-old vine grown from a rooted cutting. Before you plant, prune roots to healthy undamaged tissue; reduce the top to a single stem that is cut back to three or four buds. Then plant in a permanent place. Set a stake at once or wait until the second spring. Buds will break through the first summer to make short shoots. In February, shorten the strongest of these to three or four buds; remove the rest at the trunk. (Older pruning methods require the removal of extra shoots during the growing season.)

Through the second summer, save the strongest new shoot and cut off the rest; tie the shoot to the stake. If wires are to be used, string them at the end of this summer. Remove the vine from its stake, and secure it to the lowest wire with strips of soft cloth. Here are typical wire spacings: for a three-wire system, 2½ feet above the ground, 4½ feet, and 6 feet; for a two-wire system, 3 feet above the ground and 5½ feet. (Commercial growers favor the less expensive two-wire trellis, though three wires work better in windy places.)

In February, following the second summer, cut the vine back to a plump bud at the level of the bottom wire. (With the Kniffin system carry a very *strong* vine to the top wire.) More likely during the third summer, grow the vine up to the top wire for Kniffin training; save four side branches, two at the top and two at the bottom wires. (For the Upright system, spread two branches along the bottom wire, and allow no upright growth at all.)

By the third winter your pattern is set; a Kniffin-trained vine reaches to the top wire and has two year-old side shoots at the top and two at the bottom. The Upright system produces a vine with a trunk reaching to the bottom wire where one branch goes right and one left along the wire. Since fruit is produced on year-old wood, your job from now on is to keep a supply of bearing wood coming on. Discourage fruiting the fourth summer.

Prune the Kniffin-trained vine this way: in February cut back four year-old canes lying along the wires to one or two buds. When these buds break, save only the strongest shoot at each stub to tie along each wire; cut off the rest. The next winter, shorten these to three buds on each upper arm, four or five buds on each lower arm. Those buds will bear clusters.

PRUNING GRAPES FOR PRODUCTION. Figure 1 before pruning and Figure 2 after pruning show a mature vine trained to the four-arm Kniffin system. The arms left on the trunk in Figure 2 are year-old canes; through summer, shoots will break from the stubs left at the main trunk, and four of these will be used the next year to renew the bearing branches. Figure 3 shows a vine pruned to the Upright system; as in the Kniffin system, for annual renewal of fruiting wood, shoots are allowed to break from stubs spaced along the two arms. Figure 4 shows a young plant pruned before it is set out in the field. Figure 5 shows a detail of a flowering, year-old branch. By controlling the number of flower buds, the size and quality of the fruit can be adjusted to the strength of each vine.

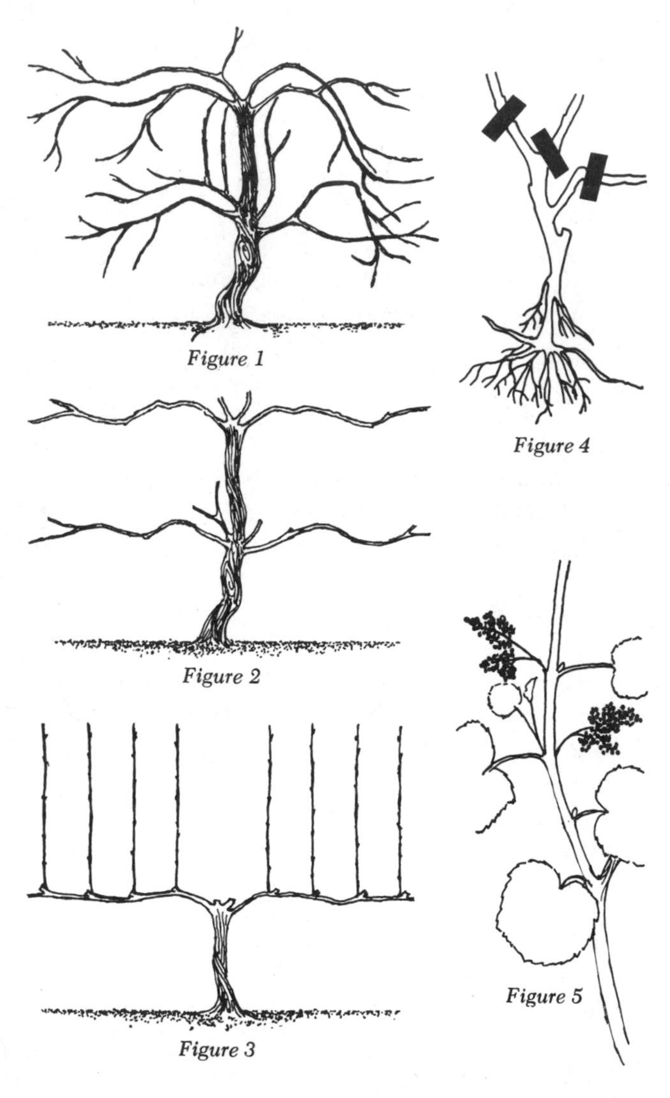

Figure 1

Figure 2

Figure 3

Figure 4

Figure 5

Prune your Upright-system vine this way: in February, select two or three well-spaced buds on each arm—let one of them be at the far end of each arm—and rub off the rest. Tie the shoots that arise from these arms straight up to the top wire. The next summer, clip off these shoots at the top wire; the buds below will bear fruit. Allow a new shoot to develop near the base of the bearing shoot to take its place the following winter. A mature vine will support from thirty to sixty fruit buds; forty is a good average.

Always bring up bearing wood from the basic branch system; don't choose a year-old shoot arising along the arm. This is where people get into trouble. They don't prune enough in midwinter. Prune your Kniffin-trained grapes to a single year-old cane arising from each short branch; prune your Upright system grapes to new canes arising from the selected points on the two lower branches. *Keep no upright wood after it has fruited.*

Pergola and trellis-grown vines may have longer trunks, heavier branches, and shorter fruiting arms. You have to decide between shade and grapes; the more old wood and vigorous new growth you keep for shade, the fewer fine grape clusters you will harvest. A good compromise is a vine tall enough to reach the top of your structure, with permanent lateral arms reaching out several feet from the main trunk, and shortened fruiting branches. Further reduce these by judicious summer pruning to keep the vine from wasting reserves on foliage.

Rotundifolias, scuppernongs, and muscadines are strong rangy vines. They are almost always pergola-grown in a rough approximation of the Kniffin four-arm system. However, a vigorous plant may be allowed up to 100 buds at the midwinter pruning.

Treat Vinifera vines differently. Gradually build up a short, sturdy trunk with a "goblet" of stubby, permanent branches at the top. Every year, let fruiting wood grow up from buds on these stubs; grapes are borne on the *new* wood. Support these vines on individual 4- to 6-foot stakes, depending on the variety. Wine sorts, as 'Zinfandel', 'Riesling', and 'Cabernet Sauvignon', are grown on a 15-inch trunk; table grapes, as 'Flame Tokay' and 'Emperor', on a 30-inch trunk. Plant, train, and prune Viniferas in this way: Plant a 14-inch rooted cutting in winter with one, not more than two, buds above ground. The first summer, allow only one stalk to develop. The next winter cut back this stalk to one, possibly two, buds and again allow only one shoot to grow.

Tie this to a stake. The third winter, stop-back the cane where the head is to be built up; the next summer, remove all side shoots except those near the top, and pinch these at 15 inches. The fourth winter cut all of these to one bud; remove those below the "crown." The next year you will have a goblet of shoots; thin these according to species and vigor. Most trunks can carry from five to fifteen stubs. Grapes are harvested beginning with the third or fourth summer.

Wafer-ash see **PTELEA trifoliata**
Wahoo see **EUONYMUS**
Walnut see **JUGLANS**
Waxberry see **SYMPHORICARPOS**
Wax-myrtle see **MYRICA**
Waxwork see **CELASTRUS**
Wayfaring-tree see **VIBURNUM**

WEIGELA MIDSUMMER

Since this blooms on new growth, prune heavily after flowering to remove most of the wood that is more than two years old. This heavy pruning keeps a good crop of basal shoots coming. These produce a trim, rather spreading shrub that is not too tall. In the North, you may have to go over your bush in late spring to remove winter-injured wood. This shrub is touchy about soil and fertility; if you give it good drainage and a winter mulch of composted barnyard manure, it looks fine; on poor or soggy soil, it is always full of dead wood and no amount of pruning will make it attractive. To renew an old specimen, cut it to the ground, mulch it heavily, keep it watered and, as new shoots appear, save only the sturdiest. Cut out spindly and crowded canes.

Whitebeam see **SORBUS**
White-forsythia see **ABELIOPHYLLUM distichum**
Whortleberry see **VACCINIUM**
Wild cherry see **PRUNUS**
Wild plum see **PRUNUS**
Willow see **SALIX**
Winterberry see **ILEX**
Wintergreen see **GAULTHERIA**
Winter-hazel see **CORYLOPSIS**

Winter savory see **SATUREJA montana**
Wintersweet see **CHIMONANTHUS praecox**
Wire-plant see **MUHLENBECKIA**

WISTERIA

SPRING-SUMMER

When you plant a young vine, prune it back to about six leaf buds or joints. Tie all shoots produced through the first summer to a strong temporary stake or trellis. Early the next spring, remove all but one or two of the strongest growths, cutting back to the main stalk. Then head-back the one or two selected canes to six or eight buds. As these buds break, allow only one of the uppermost ones to develop into a vine; prune off or pinch back vining shoots from the other buds, but leave the cluster of foliage that developed before the vining. Flowers will be produced on year-old wood that comes from the spurlike bushy growth at each joint along the cane. Severe spring thinning of old wood and continuous summer pinching of new growth produce ornamental vines and abundant bloom.

You can recondition ancient vines by sawing off old wood right to the ground. To rebuild the plant, save and train up one or two of the basal shoots that are thinner than your thumb. Sever surface or subsurface runners that spread for yards around the base of the plant and pull them out of the ground. Or you can prune old wood to an open ornamental bush form. Cut back trunks to a convenient height and remove all but a few well-spaced branches; cut these back. A gnarled and contorted free-standing plant will result. Allow only a tuft of foliage to develop here and there so that trunks are featured. Flowers will eventually develop from the foliage-bearing branchlets.

When you set out a standard (tree-form) plant, prune severely. Just as buds begin to show green, rub off all but two or three on each branch. Pinch back vining growth that pushes out beyond the first cluster of leaves, but let the leaf clusters remain to clothe the plant and make food for stem and roots. Provide a strong stake when you plant, and replace the stake as needed through the first ten years. To keep a plant well braced, after the first year, cut back new growth to one or two well-spaced joints. Remove entirely weak and in-growing shoots. To develop shapely, well-furnished specimens with neat, tight heads, prune standards severely and frequently throughout the growing season.

From young and old vines or standards, cut out basal sprouts with

TRAINING A YOUNG WISTERIA VINE. Here is a well-pruned specimen as it appears in early spring when new shoots are just breaking. Note the absence of criss-crossing and tangled growth, and the scars on each shoot where it was headed back last summer. The vine is kept under the support wires and branches are spaced to avoid crowding; even so, when the foliage is fully expanded, this panel of wall will be almost completely covered. *Author photo*

a sharp knife as soon as they appear. Almost all nursery-grown plants are grafted so growth arising from below the graft is a threat to desirable top wood. When plants don't bloom, restrict new growth to one leaf bud; cut out all weak viny wood at the point where it breaks from a heavier stem; rub off green buds near the base. Don't root-prune to force bloom; an injured root system will send up sprouts for yards around.

Witch-hazel see **HAMAMELIS**

Wormwood see **ARTEMISIA**
Yew see **TAXUS**
Youngberry see **RUBUS**
Yulan see **MAGNOLIA**

ZANTHOXYLUM PRICKLY-ASH, HERCULES-CLUB LATE WINTER

Prune as needed to make this fit the place in which it grows. You may wish to drastically thin out branches so as to feature the blunt rather heavy limbs, or to keep them cut back, thus developing a bush of stout unbranched sprouts heavily armed with vicious thorns. My preference is to prune it to the ground and put salt on the stumps to finish it off, but perhaps you can take advantage of the thorny bushy habit to discourage foot traffic somewhere.

ZELKOVA SUMMER

Prune seedlings to one shoot and, until they are shoulder high, keep them so, nipping off side branches at the end of summer. Let alone, they will either form half a dozen leaders or develop into a small thorn-tree like a prairie hawthorn. Young trees are twiggy, tending to branch laterally and to form a round top; keep cutting to a leader and eventually your tree will resume upward growth to become a towering giant that needs little or no pruning. The first twenty years are the hardest! Small trees may be potted up to grow as bonsai subjects. Pinch back all new growth to one or two leaves but have in mind maintaining a dominant leader. Eventually this makes an excellent dwarf tree to train in the Japanese manner.

ZIZYPHUS JUJUBE SUMMER

Prune young trees to a single leader; as they reach 4 to 5 feet, allow side branches to form but head them back by pinching soft tips. Keep trees growing upright as long as possible, but don't trim them formally as their beauty lies in a zigzag form of branches with tailored foliage and glossy wooden-looking fruits. Thin out enough so each branch is featured in its own right.

Some DO'S and DON'TS

DO

Keep pruning tools sharp and well oiled; use the right tool for the job.

Prune with a definite reason and purpose.

Have in mind time of bloom and age of flower-producing wood.

Carry hand-pruners about with you for the inevitable little jobs that save big jobs later.

Prune weak or failing plants hard; strong growers lightly if space permits.

Prune flush to branch or trunk. If only the end of a branch is dead, cut just below and close to a leaf bud but be sure the branch is dead—not dormant. Check for green wood by skinning away the bark with your fingernail or knife.

Cut off a diseased, dead, or broken branch *at any time.*

Prune off the weaker of two rubbing or interfering branches that are producing bark wounds—the quicker the better.

Prune tip branches to produce a low spreading tree—prune lateral or side branches to make a tree grow upward and be less bushy.

Cover cuts over 1 inch across with tree-wound dressing.

Prune hedge plants wider at base than top.

DON'T

Don't try to prune with dull, sprung, or the wrong tools.

Don't leave stubs, ragged cuts, or torn bark; use sharp cutting tools.

Don't prune spring-flowering shrubs in fall, winter, or spring, but right after flowering.

Don't count on pruning to keep naturally tall plants low or broad plants narrow, especially in foundation groups.

For high pruning avoid dangerous positions on a box or chair. Keep your feet on the ground and cut with long-handled pruners or long-reach extension tree-pruners.

Don't climb trees; for big high-up jobs, get a professional tree-man who has proper training, skill, and equipment.

Seasonal Guide

Late winter into early spring. Remove at the ground line a few of the oldest canes from all mature shrubs *except the early flowering ones.*

Trim deciduous hedges to insure a form rather wide at base, rather narrow at top.

Prune dormant fruit trees, remove weak and crossing or interfering branches; thin and head-back twigs carrying flower buds; get rid of all water sprouts on trunks.

On flowering and ornamental trees, cut off any inconvenient low branches or those that rub or grow crosswise within the trees.

Do not prune shade trees and evergreens at this time.

Late spring into early summer. Remove a few of the oldest canes on mature shrubs that have bloomed; take off flowers as soon as they fade; stop-back young wood enough to encourage branching.

Once new growth starts, freely trim evergreens. To restrict size of pines, hemlock, spruce, and some other needle trees, remove half or more of new growth *before* needles fully expand and harden. To reduce size of junipers, take off all of last year's growth, cutting back to a branchlet that grows parallel to the branch you are removing.

As new canes appear, pinch out tips of flowering shrubs to encourage branching.

Remove dead flowers on azaleas and rhododendrons to prevent formation of unsightly seed pods; pinch back the new shoots to keep plants dense and shapely.

Throughout the summer. Shear hedges regularly as indicated by a ragged appearance, keeping the lower part wider than the top. From time to time remove entire branches from deep inside evergreens growing at the foundation of your house or in the garden. To maintain constant size, the trick is to force a continuous renewal of branches, especially on Pfitzer junipers and their relatives.

Remove a few lower branches each summer from *young* shade trees to develop clear tall trunks; if a side or lateral branch threatens to weaken or dominate the main shoot—the leader of the tree—cut out the side branch so that the leader maintains proper dominance. Old-timers claim that summer pruning restricts growth, winter pruning stimulates it. Experience bears this out. Heavily prune a flowering crabapple tree in winter and, come spring, it will be a mass of water sprouts; prune it severely in the summer and it will grow dense, and the sprouts that do appear can easily be rubbed off while still in the bud stage.

Make it a habit to pinch tips out of leafy shoots as you walk around the garden; this will make your trees and shrubs grow thicker and be better looking. Of course, do not pinch out tips of plants that have not bloomed or you will remove the flower buds that are yet to open.

Fall into winter. Ease off pruning of evergreens in fall. Work over shrubs once more particularly to get rid of basal suckers. Prune shade trees throughout the winter.

Index

Botanical names and all the common names of plants that are treated in this book are included in the alphabetical listing, pages 58 to 185. Therefore, only the principal common names and the botanical names that have additional references are listed here. Illustrations are indicated by heavy type.

Actinidia, Chinese, 64
Alder, 65
Almond, 149–50
Alphabetical list of Plants, 58–185
Andromeda, 143
Annuals, 24
Antarctic-beech, 136
Apple, 14, 15, 46, **52,** 131, **132, 133**
Apricot, flowering, 148–49
Arborvitae, 14, 46, 171
  globe, 53
Ash, 112–13
Aster, 48
Aucuba, Japanese, 72
Avocado, 140–41
Azalea, 13, 42, **47,** 72, **73**
Bald-cypress, 170
Bamboo, 142
Barberry, 73
Bark, **19,** 26, **35, 36,** 44
Basswood, 171–72
Bayberry, 135
Beauty-berry, 79
Beauty-bush, 124
Beech, **75,** 108–09
Birch, 46, 74
  weeping, 18
  white, **9,** 14, **75**
Bittersweet, 83–84
Bladder-nut, 166
Bladder-senna, 94
Bluebeard, 81–82
Blueberry, 173–74, **174**
Bonsai, 49, 54–55
Bottle-brush, 79
Boxwood, **20, 53,** 78
Brambles, 160–62
Bridal-wreath, 165–66
Broom, 100, 113
Buckthorn, 154
Bud dominance, 43–44
Buds, 20, **25,** 42
  importance of, in pruning, 20, **23,** 41–42, **59**
  latent, 25, 31–32, 42
  structure of, **22,** 41
Buffalo-berry, 164
Bull-bay, 130
Burning-bush, 107–08
Bush fruits, 42, 46
Bush-arbutus, 60
Bush-clover, 126
Bush-honeysuckle, 102–03
Butternut, 122
Button-bush, 85
Calamondin, 90–91
California-lilac, 82–83
Cambium tissue, 19, 20, 21, 26, 44
Candytuft, hardy, 120
Cane (Bamboo), 71
Cane fruits, 15
Canes, 25, **59**
Cape-plumbago, 144
Carolina allspice, 80

Catalpa, 31, 82
Ceanothus, 49, 82
Cedar, 83, **84**
Chaste-tree, 177–78
Checker-berry, 113
Cherry, 146–47
  flowering, 148–49
  wild, **75,** 148
Cherry-laurel, 150
Chestnut, 82
Chinaberry-tree, 134
Chokeberry, 21, 70
Christmas-berry, 142
Chrysanthemum, 48
Cinquefoil, 146
Clematis, 15, 91–93, **92**
Clippers, **28, 38**
Columbine, 47
Coppice, 31
Coral-tree, 106–07
Coral-vine, 68
Cordon, 18, 33, 49, 52
Cork-tree, 141
Cotoneaster, 49, 98
Crabapple, 56, 131–34
  flowering, 33, 44
Crape-myrtle, 124–25
Cross-vine, 74
Croton, 94
Crowberry, 104
Crown, 12, 17, 46
Cryptomeria, 55
Currant, 154–55
Cypress, 99–100
Dahlia, 100, **101**
Daisy, Michaelmas, 48
Dards, 32
Dehorning, 30
Delphinium, **47**
Deutzia, 102
Devil's-walking-stick, 68
Do's and don'ts in pruning, 186
Dogwood, **14,** 33, 47, **75**
Douglas-fir, 151
Dove-tree, 102
Drop pruning, 14, **19,** 26–30, **37,** 42
Dutchman's-pipe, 70
Elderberry, 162–63
Elm, **16,** 20, 46, 55, **156,** 172–73
Empress-tree, 140
Ericaceous plants, 13
Espalier-trained trees, 18, 49–52
  Lorette pruning for, 31
  root pruning for, 33, 51
Euonymus, 16, **20**
  Japanese, 48
Evergreens. *See* Shrubs, evergreen; Trees, evergreen.
False-buckthorn, 78
False-cypress, 87
False-spirea, 165
Fans, 49
Fir, 16, 43, 61
Firethorn, 152
Five-leaf akebia, 65
Five-leaf aralia, 61
Flowering-maple, 61
Forsythia, 7, 21, 24, 25, 49, 110–12, **110, 111**
Foundation planting, **47**
Fringe-tree, 88, **89**
Fruit. *See* Bush fruits; Cane fruits, Fruit trees; also specific names of fruits, such as Apple, Blueberry, etc.
Fruit trees, 7, 8, 15, 56, **147**
  cordon, 18
difference between flower and fruit buds of, 42
  dwarf, 18, 49
  espalier-trained, 18, 49–51
  Lorette pruning for, 31–32
  pruning schedule for, 46
  reworking of old, **34, 36**
  root pruning for, 33
Giant-reed, 71
Goldenchain-tree, 124
Golden-glow, 48
Goldenrain-tree, 124
Gotelli Collection, 54
Grape, 15, 178–82, **180**
  difference between flower and fruit buds of, 42
Grapefruit, 90–91
Guelder-rose, 175
Hackberry, 55, 85
Hand-pruner, 21, **32,** 38
Hardy-orange, 145
Hawthorn, 99
Hazelnut, 96–97
Heartwood, **19**
Heath, 105
Heather, 13, 79
Heavenly-bamboo, 135–36
Hedge, 7, 8, 13, 17, **20**
Hedge sheers, **28,** 38, 53
Hedge-thorn, 80–81
Helenium, 48
Hemlock, 21, 172
Hercules-club, 185
Hickory, 81
Holly, 42, 120–21
  American, **25**

Holly (continued)
  Japanese, 16
Hollyhock, 47
Holly-olive, 138
Honey-locust, 114
Honeysuckle, 15, 127-28
Hop-hornbeam, 138
Horse-chestnut, 20, 26, 64, **156**
Hydrangea, 117–19, **118**
Internode, **25**, 41
Irish-heath, 100
Ivy, 15, **45**, 116
Japanese-cedar, 99
Jasmine, 121–22
Jessamine, 86
Jetbead, 154
Jujube, 185
Juniper, 46, 55, 122–23
  Pfitzer, 8, 18, **27**, 30
  spreading, 14, **27**
Katsura-tree, 85–86
Kentucky coffee-tree, 115
Larch, 125
Laurel, mountain-, 13, 123
Lavender, 125
Lavender-cotton, 163
Leader, 16, 21, **27**
Leadplant, 66
Lemon, 90–91
Leucothöe, 126
Lilac, 8, 12, 21, 168–70, **169**
Limbs, removal of, 25–26
Lime (*Citrus*), 90–91
Lime (*Tilia*), 171–72
Linden, 26, 171
Locust, 155, **156**
Lopper, **28**, 36
Loquat, 105, **106**
Lorette pruning, 31–32, 46
Lythrum, 48
Madagascar-jasmine, 166–67
Madrona, 69
Magnolia, **43**
Maidenhair-tree, 114
Maintenance pruning, 7–10
Mallow, 116–17
Manzanita, 69
Maple, 26, 46, 55, 56, 62–64
Matrimony-vine, 128
Mexican-orange, 88
Mock-orange, 141–42
Monkey-puzzle tree, 68–69
Monkshood-vine, 67
Mountain-ash, 165
Mountain-laurel, 123
Mulberry, 46, 134–35
Myrtle, 48, 135
National Arboretum, 54
New-Jersey-tea, 82–83
Ninebark, 142
Node, **25**
Oak, 153
Oleander, 136
Oleaster, 104
Olive, 137
Orange, 90–91
Oregon-grape, 130–31
Osage-orange, 130
Overcut, 26, 30, **36**
Pagoda-tree, Japanese, 44–46, 164–65
Paper-mulberry, 76
Passion-flower, 139–40
Paste dressing, 38
Pawpaw, 71
Peach, 150–51
Pear, 31–32, 46, **49**, 152–53
Pearl-bush, 108
Pecan, 81
Peegee, 117–19, **118**
Peony, 139
Perennials, 24, 47–48
Persimmon, 103
Petunia, 7
Phlox, summer, 48
Pigeon-berry, 103
Pinching, 24–25, **32**, 47–48
Pine, 16, 21, **27**, 43, 46, 55, 143
  Austrian, **11**
Pleaching, 14, 31
Plum, 148, 149
Plum-yew, 85
Poinsettia, 108
Pollarding, 31
Pomegranate, dwarf, 152
Pond-cypress, 170
Poplar, 14, 145–46
  Lombardy, 18
Portugese-laurel, 53
Prickly-ash, 185
Privet, 8, 13, 53, 126
Pruning
  A to Z of, 58–185
  by trenching, 33–34
  do's and don'ts of, 186
  drop pruning, 26–30
  importance of buds in, 20, **58**
  in warm climates, 48
  Lorette, 31–32, 46
  maintenance, 7–10
  methods, 17–40
  reasons for, 7–16, 17
  removing large limbs, 26, **36**

Pruning (continued)
root, 32–33
seasonal guide for, 41, 46, 187–88
special techniques, 30–32, 49–57
structure as guide to, **19, 86**
three steps in, 10
to control size and shape, 59, 156
to correct unbalanced growth, 16
to recondition (rework) neglected plants, 11–15, 24
to restore damaged plants, 15–16
Pruning knife, **29, 38**
Pruning tools and supplies, **28, 29, 34,** 35–40, **36, 37, 39**
care of, 38–40, 186
warning about use of, 21–22
Pyracantha, 49, 52
Queen's creeper, 141
Quince, 49, 86
Raspberry, 160–62, **161**
Rat-stripper, 138–39
Reconditioning plants, 11–15, 24
Redbud, 33, 86
Redwood, 164
Remedial pruning, 15–16
Rhododendron, 13, 24, **47, 73,** 154
Rock-rose, 90
Root pruning, **19,** 32–33, 34, 35, 46
Roots, **19,** 21, 42
Rootstock, 49
Rose, 7, 8, 12, 20, 155–60
bush, **158**
climbing, **159**
Rosemary, 53
St.-John's-wort, 119–20
Sapwood, **19**
Saws, pruning, 23, **29, 34, 36, 37, 39**
Scholar-tree, Chinese, 164–65
Seasonal pruning guide, 41, 46, 187–88
Secateur, **28,** 38
Shadblow, 66
Shrubs, 12, 26, 30, 34, 56, **59**
espalier-trained, 49, 51, 52
evergreen, 30, 46, 47, 51
flowering, 10–13, 17–18, 30, 49, 52, **177, 178**
Silk-oak, 114–15
Silktree, Japanese, 65
Silverbell-tree, 115
Smoke-tree, 97–98
Snowball, 117–19, **118**
Snowberry, 168
Snow-in-summer, 134
Sorrel-tree, 138
Sour gum, 33, 136
Southernwood, 70–71
Spice-bush, 127
Spruce, 16, 21, 43, 55, 142–43
Spurge-laurel, 102
Spurs, 51
Stipular eyes, 31, 32
Structure as guide to pruning
of buds and twigs, **22, 23, 25,** 41
of tree, **19, 75, 86, 156**
Suckers, 10, 13
Sumac, 154
Summer-lilac, 77–78
Sweet-box, 163
Sweet-gum-tree, 127
Sweetleaf, 168
Sweet-pepperbush, 93
Sweetshade, 119
Sycamore, 14, 31, 144
Tamarisk, 170
Thigmotropism, 16
Thinning, 30
Tipu-tree, 172
Tomato, 128, **129**
Topiary pruning, 49, 52–54, **53, 54**
Tracing back (out), 14, **35**
Tree-of-Heaven, 64
Trees, 13, 18, 44–46, 54, 55, **156**. *See also* specific names, as Dogwood.
Trees, evergreen, 13, 14, 16, 18, 21, **27,** 30, 33, 43, 46, 51, 55, 56
Tree-wound dressing, 26, **29, 35,** 38
Trench pruning, 33–34
Trumpet-creeper, 15, 80
Tulip-tree, 127
Twigs, **21, 22, 23**
Umbrella-pine, 163–64
Undercut, 26, 30, **36**
Understock, 12, 33
Veronica, 116
Viburnum, 20, 21, 49, **175, 176**
Vines, 15
Virginia-creeper, 139
Virgin's-bower, 91–93
Vitex, **177, 178**
Walnut, 46, 122
Wafer-ash, 151
White-forsythia, 60
Willow, 162
Winter savory, 163
Winter-hazel, 96
Wintersweet, 87
Wire-plant, 135
Wisteria, 13, 15, 183, **184**
Witch-hazel, 115
Wood, 10, 12, **19, 59**
Yellowwood, 14
Yew, 13, 14, 30, 42, 46, 49, 53, 170–71